Beginning
Land Law

Whether you're new to higher education, coming to legal study for the first time or just wondering what Land Law is all about, **Beginning Land Law** is the ideal introduction to help you hit the ground running. Starting with the basics and an overview of each topic, it will help you come to terms with the structure, themes and issues of the subject so that you can begin your Land Law module with confidence.

Adopting a clear and simple approach with legal vocabulary carefully clarified, Sarah King breaks the subject of Land Law down using practical everyday examples to make it understandable for anyone, whatever their background. Diagrams and flowcharts simplify complex issues, important cases are identified and explained and on-the-spot questions help you recognise potential issues or debates within the law so that you can contribute in classes with confidence.

Beginning Land Law is an ideal first introduction to the subject for LLB, GDL or ILEX students and especially international students, those enrolled on distance learning courses or on other degree programmes.

Sarah King is Academic Practice Advisor at the University of Birmingham.

Beginning the Law

A new introductory series designed to help you master the basics and progress with confidence.

Beginning Constitutional Law, Nick Howard
Beginning Contract Law, Nicola Monaghan and Chris Monaghan
Beginning Criminal Law, Claudia Carr and Maureen Johnson
Beginning Equity and Trusts, Mohamed Ramjohn
Beginning Employment Law, James Marson
Beginning Evidence, Chanjit Singh Landa
Beginning Human Rights, Howard Davis
Beginning Family Law, Jonathan Herring
Beginning Business Law, Chris Monaghan
Beginning Land Law, Sarah King

Following in Spring 2015
Beginning Medical Law, Claudia Carr

www.routledge.com/cw/beginningthelaw

Beginning
Land Law

SARAH KING

Routledge
Taylor & Francis Group

LONDON AND NEW YORK

First published 2015
by Routledge
2 Park Square, Milton Park, Abingdon, Oxon OX14 4RN

and by Routledge
711 Third Avenue, New York, NY 10017

Routledge is an imprint of the Taylor & Francis Group, an informa business

© 2015 Sarah King

The right of Sarah King to be identified as author of this work
has been asserted by her in accordance with sections 77 and 78
of the Copyright, Designs and Patents Act 1988.

All rights reserved. No part of this book may be reprinted or
reproduced or utilised in any form or by any electronic, mechanical,
or other means, now known or hereafter invented, including photocopying
and recording, or in any information storage or retrieval system,
without permission in writing from the publishers.

Trademark notice: Product or corporate names may be trademarks
or registered trademarks, and are used only for identification
and explanation without intent to infringe.

British Library Cataloguing in Publication Data
A catalogue record for this book is available from the British Library

Library of Congress Cataloging in Publication Data has been requested

ISBN: 978-1-138-02176-1 (hbk)
ISBN: 978-1-138-02175-4 (pbk)
ISBN: 978-1-315-77753-5 (ebk)

Typeset in Vectora
by Florence Production Ltd, Stoodleigh, Devon, UK

Printed and bound by CPI Group (UK) Ltd, Croydon, CR0 4YY

Contents

Table of Cases

Table of Legislation

Preface

My approach to teaching land law over the last decade has been to provide my students with a way into the subject that allows them to make connections with their own experience, breaks down complex topics into manageable pieces and gives them confidence to reinforce and develop their learning both in class with the teaching team and independently through their own research.

My aim in writing *Beginning Land Law* has been to try to re-create this approach through a textbook that gives you an introduction to this subject, with opportunities to reflect on and test your early learning and a foundation on which to build with your further studies. The book is supported by an online resource centre that offers you suggested thinking points related to the on-the-spot questions, links to additional resources and a glossary of key terms.

I would like to thank Fiona Briden at Routledge and Damian Mitchell for all their support as I have been writing this book. I would also like to thank my colleagues and all my students in the Law School at Birmingham City University who have made teaching land law so enjoyable. Finally, I would like to thank my family, Mark, Olivia and Sophie, for their encouragement and patience.

Sarah King
Birmingham City University
Sarah King is a former Solicitor and Senior Lecturer in the Law School at Birmingham City University. She is now Academic Practice Advisor at the University of Birmingham.

www.routledge.com/cw/beginningthelaw

Visit the *Beginning the Law* website to discover a comprehensive range of resources designed to enhance your learning experience.

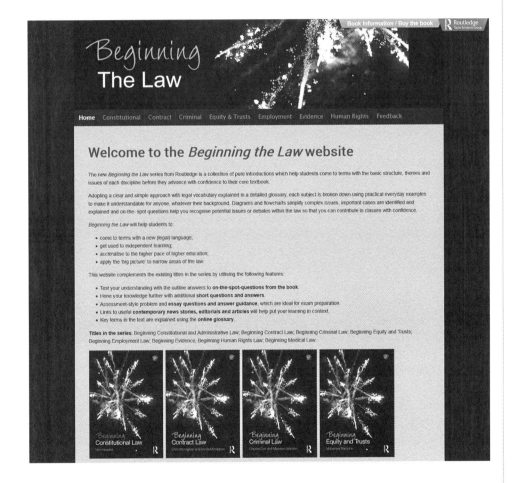

Answers to on-the-spot questions

The author's suggested answers to the questions posed in the book.

Online glossary

Reinforce your legal vocabulary with our online glossary. You can find easy to remember definitions of all key terms, listed by chapter for each title in the *Beginning the Law* series.

Chapter 1

An introduction to land law

A very brief guide to studying land law

INTRODUCTION

Many students begin their studies of land law with a certain degree of trepidation. It has a reputation as a challenging subject, one perhaps that even has the potential to be a little dry. The reality, though, is very different. Land law is a dynamic subject and one that will touch every single one of us in our lifetime. You might have aspirations to own your own home one day, you might already be thinking of buying a house and are researching a mortgage. You might as you read this be thinking about negotiating a new tenancy agreement with the landlord of your student house, or perhaps even be in dispute with a neighbour about a boundary. The fact is that land and its associated rights and responsibilities are all around us and the law that regulates the ownership and use of land is of vital importance to our society.

From a career perspective you might also want to reconsider any preconceived ideas about land law. The study of this subject opens up opportunities that might include working in real estate in a variety of ways. Most people buying a home will instruct a solicitor; many corporate support roles relate to property aspects of transactions. You might be acting for residential developers or commercial landlords or tenants. You may not even be a lawyer but find that an understanding of land law is an advantage, as a surveyor for example.

For all of these reasons you should approach the study of land law with an open mind. If you approach this textbook in the same way you will gain an understanding of some of the basic principles on which you can build with your subsequent study. In this book the aim is to encourage you to engage with some of the key concepts in relation to land law and to offer a way in to studying the subject that will build your confidence in this area. We do this by introducing concepts in a very structured way and using modern examples to bring the legal concepts to life.

This book is primarily written for those who have no prior knowledge of land law who are looking for an introduction to the subject before developing their learning with more detailed textbooks and materials. It will be useful to students embarking on studies in law as well as students studying non-law degrees who might need an introduction to legal aspects of their course (students studying on real estate, planning or surveying courses, for example). The book may also be useful for those who want a land law refresher, perhaps before commencing postgraduate study or training in this area.

CONTENT

The content reflects the introductory nature of the book and focuses on the key topics that are likely to be covered by a land law curriculum. The early chapters of the book offer an introduction to the foundations of land law. They introduce land as a form of property, looking at how we define land in a practical and legal sense and the implications of this for study. You will quickly understand that land is not just something that is tangible, the ground that we walk on or even the house that we live in. It also includes the intangible rights that are associated with it, for example the rights that allow us to walk over land that we do not otherwise own. These chapters also introduce you to the basic practice of buying and selling land and creating interests in relation to it by reference to the two main systems for land ownership, registered and unregistered land. Some of the concepts that relate to these two systems are complex but they are presented in a clear and structured way with lots of reference to examples to enable you to make connections with your own experience and aspects of modern life with which we are all familiar. By taking this approach you will recognise the value and importance of the concepts introduced and will be able to apply these to the chapters that follow.

The remaining chapters of the book look at key topics in relation to land law that will appear in most law courses. They include introductions to the ways in which ownership rights in land can be acquired. Some of these are acquired formally, for example through the vehicle of a lease (covered in Chapter 6) or the purchase of a freehold by co-owners (covered in Chapter 5). Others are acquired informally, for example squatters rights acquired through the legal mechanism known as adverse possession (covered in Chapter 7). They will also include explanations and discussions of how third parties might acquire rights in relation to land, for example how a lender acquires their interest through a mortgage (covered in Chapter 10) or how a person might be granted a right of way (covered by an introduction to easements in Chapter 8).

The content of all of the chapters is intended to be introductory, offering you a 'way in' to the subject and a basis on which to build with further reading and study. The intention is to present the concepts in an accessible way and not to rely on legal terminology that may not be familiar to you. Key terms are defined and a more detailed glossary is available through the companion website. The most important cases are introduced with brief reference to facts, decisions and principles and the relevance of these cases to your learning is highlighted. Where appropriate, we use visual aids to illustrate the key points. On-the-spot questions invite you to think more deeply about some of the points of law and make connections with learning and experience acquired elsewhere. Support, suggestions and points to think about in relation to these questions will be available via the companion website.

APPROACHES TO LEARNING

There is no escaping the fact that the study of land law can be challenging. It takes a little while to familiarise yourself with some of the terminology and concepts so be patient. Some of the law is historic, occasionally convoluted and sometimes ripe for reform. Understanding where the law has come from and how it has developed will help with this. Similarly understanding why there needs to be change and the proposals for reform will help you to understand the principles. That is why some of the suggested additional reading can be accessed easily and freely online via the Law Commission or Land Registry.

Our suggested approach to studying land law is to break down the concepts, principles and issues into manageable pieces. By starting with the basics and building them up you will develop confidence in the subject and will be ready to supplement your understanding with more complex and challenging thinking. Chapter 9, for example, covers the complex area of land law known as freehold covenants. This is a perfect example of law that has developed from historic common law rules that were subsequently supplemented and softened by the intervention of equitable rules making it complex and unwieldy. It is an area of land law that has been the subject of much criticism for a number of years and, many would argue, is in urgent need of reform.

If you work through Chapter 9 methodically you will quickly grasp the basics. The early on-the-spot question is designed to get you thinking about the nature of covenants and their relevance in a modern context by inviting you to imagine that you are buying a house on a new estate. The thinking that flows from this will help you to understand how and why covenants are used by lawyers in the practice of buying and selling property. We build on this by explaining the contractual nature of covenants, drawing on your knowledge and experience of basic contract law and then encouraging you to think about the different types of covenants that could be created.

As the law becomes more complex you can then use another example to think through some of the potential difficulties in enforcing covenants against people who may not originally have agreed to the terms of the contractual promise that was made. We then introduce the law that determines whether it is possible to enforce covenants against these non-contracting parties. A visual aid is included to help you to do this in a structured way and reference is made back to the example to help you to make sense of the principles. Gradually, you are building up your knowledge and understanding of the topic of covenants to a point where you recognise the key legal principles and from there you are ready to begin to apply them to legal problems, critically evaluate their purpose and analyse the need to reform through further study and research. As a starting point for this we point you in the direction of some early further reading. In relation to covenants this includes a link to the Law Commission, whose report *Making Land Work: Easements, Covenants and Profits à Prendre*, which is freely available online, contains their detailed proposals for reform in this area.

Remember that this is an introductory book and is not intended to be a complete work on land law. You will be provided with reading lists on your own courses that will supplement and develop the law that is introduced here. You should also make an effort to read both the primary and secondary sources of law in this area. Reading cases and statutes as well as journal articles that review them is a valuable way of learning and often provides the detail and analysis that will support and enhance your reading of textbooks.

ANSWERING QUESTIONS ON LAND LAW

A detailed consideration of the ways in which land law might be assessed as a subject is outside the scope of this book but generally the format of the types of questions that might be asked, whether in an exam, coursework or portfolio approach, will fall into two categories – essay or problem based.

Problem-based questions are generally all about application of the law that you have learned. As suggested earlier in this introduction, before you can apply the law you need to understand it and be able to explain and interpret it. Learning the basics is, therefore, crucial. Equally important is that you also take some time to understand the nature of the problem that is being presented and the issues that it raises. Rushing into a problem question without first identifying the relevant facts and issues can end up in you producing an answer that does not directly relate to the problem set. In exactly the same way that a client would not appreciate their solicitor offering advice that does not deal with the problem that they presented, so an answer that does not address the correct legal issues will lose marks.

Often there is no right or wrong answer to a problem-based question. Your ability to answer the question well will depend on your demonstration of higher level academic skills. These may include the ability to compare and contrast the decisions in relevant cases and apply them to the facts of the problem, to evaluate the relevance of a particular statutory provision and ultimately to apply individual thought based on your analysis and propose a solution or outcome. This is where beginning with the basics and building on them with more detailed reading and research will help you.

As with problem-based questions, essays require you to read and digest the question carefully before attempting an answer. There may not be a problem to solve but rather an analysis of a particular area of law or a discussion and evaluation of proposals for reform (the complex area of freehold covenants and the need for review of the law might be an example). There is always a danger with essay questions that an answer ends up being discursive, demonstrating the basic skills of knowledge and understanding of the law but failing to demonstrate higher level skills of critical thinking and evaluation. It is important with an essay question that these skills are still evident, that you demonstrate your wider reading and research and offer some form of conclusion to the question asked.

KEY SOURCES

Your course team will help you to identify the key sources for your reading and research and you may well have access to a number of online resources as well as hard copy material in the library. There are a number of good land law textbooks and many are written to suit different learning styles, some favouring more visual approaches, others giving plenty of examples or taking a question and answer approach. As suggested in this introduction, as well as identifying good textbooks to support your study you should endeavour to read primary sources of land law. Reading the judgments in key cases often gives you an insight into the discussion and debate that took place before a decision was made. Reading the detailed facts of a case helps you to make sense of the issues and seeing how the courts applied the law can really help you to develop these skills yourself.

Reading journal articles can also be a useful way to help you to understand the importance of cases and statute and to learn about how decisions and judgments have been received and critically reviewed. Again, your course team will help you to decide which journals are relevant to your course but the following might be a useful starting point:

- The Conveyancer and Property Lawyer
- Modern Law Review
- Law Quarterly Review
- Cambridge Law Journal.

There is also lots of information freely available online. In particular the Land Registry website is a particularly good reference point and helps to make connections between the academic law and practice. The following are useful links:

www.landregistry.gov.uk/ – the main Land Registry website from where you can access a number of publicly available guidance notes.

http://lawcommission.justice.gov.uk/ – this is the home page for the Law Commission. From here you can access proposals for reform to the law – including in relation to easements and covenants.

www.legislation.gov.uk/ – from here you can access all United Kingdom legislation.

Finally you may find it useful to look at some of the companion books in the Beginning the Law series. In particular *Beginning Equity and Trusts* and *Beginning Contract Law* will be useful reference points when you are considering some of the topics in this book. As you approach the end of your studies in land law you might also find it useful to refer to Routledge's Optimize series. *Optimise Land Law* is a particularly good way of starting to build on your knowledge with application of and critical reflection on the law in readiness for assessment.

Chapter 2
The foundations of land law

LEARNING OBJECTIVES

After reading this chapter, you should be able to:

- recognise and appreciate the importance of land law;
- explain, in general terms, the nature of property rights and estates in land;
- distinguish between legal and equitable rights in land;
- identify the appropriate rules for the creation of property rights.

INTRODUCTION

In beginning a study of land law you may already have a preconceived idea of what the subject is all about. A quick search on the internet comes up with definitions such as 'the part of the earth's surface that is not covered by water' (Oxford Dictionary online). If we were explaining the concept of land to someone else we might describe the ground that we walk on or perhaps a sense of open space, rural land and the countryside.

If we look up a legal definition of land, however, the position is much more complicated and, you might at first think, off-putting even. Land is defined in s.205(1)(ix) of the Law of Property Act 1925, set out overleaf. The definition broadens our understanding of what land is in a legal sense and requires us to consider more than just the physical, visible elements of land as we already understand them. The definition is complicated and some of the terms used ('advowson' for example) are largely of historic interest only. The aim of this chapter is to provide you with a knowledge of the foundations of land law and the basis from which to build your knowledge through the remainder of this book and your further reading and study of the subject.

Key definition: Land

'Land' includes land of any tenure, and mines and minerals, whether or not held apart from the surface, buildings or parts of buildings (whether the division is horizontal, vertical or made in any other way) and other corporeal hereditaments; also a manor, an advowson, and a rent and other incorporeal hereditaments, and an easement, right, privilege, or benefit in, over, or derived from land.

Law of Property Act 1925, s.205(1)(ix)

LAND AS A FORM OF PROPERTY

When we talk about property we generally mean things that are capable of belonging to or being owned by an individual or individuals. We all of us own property of some form or other, whether it is a land law textbook, mobile phone, a car or indeed a house. Our ownership of these items gives us the right to deal with them in certain ways. So we can loan our textbook to a friend, use our mobile phone to book a restaurant, sell our car when we no longer need it. We take all this for granted but our ability to act in this way stems from the fact that as owners of property we acquire rights that allow us to do this. If you think about this from another perspective it makes sense that the student who borrowed the textbook does not, themselves, acquire the right to loan it on or sell it to someone else. If we need to get the textbook back we can simply ask the student to return it. On the other hand once your car is sold you no longer have an entitlement to use it. Your rights in relation to the car have passed to someone else. In the former case the property in the textbook remains with the owning student. In the latter case the property in the car has passed to the buyer.

On-the-spot question

 Think about the types of property that you might own. What rights do you think you have in relation to that property? Are you entitled to deal with it or dispose of it in any way you like or are there restrictions on what you can do?

Land is a particular type of property. In fact it is a very special type of property that, because of its importance, has special rules attached to it. Land, in the physical sense, is a finite resource and a valuable asset (your house, for example, is likely to be the most valuable thing that you own). For that reason it is treated separately to other types of property and is often referred to as 'real property' rather than 'personal property' (the latter being a term that would encompass our examples of the textbook, phone and car).

Land as tangible and intangible property

If we look again at the statutory definition of land we can broadly split this into two parts. The first talks about land in the physical sense, as we would normally understand it. We will come back to the meaning of 'tenure' shortly but this part of the definition includes as land the surface of land, mines and minerals below the surface and buildings or parts of buildings above the surface. There is also reference to 'corporeal hereditaments', which extends the definition to any tangible object related to the land that is capable of being inherited. Examples might be boundary walls or trees.

Key definitions

Hereditament: something that is capable of being inherited.

Corporeal hereditament: a tangible object.

Incorporeal hereditament: an intangible right.

The second part of the definition is less obvious. Some of the terminology used (a manor and an advowson for example) is archaic and rarely encountered in practice, but the reference to incorporeal hereditaments and easements, rights and privileges is important. This extends the definition of land to intangible rights that relate to the land. In other words, things that are not immediately visible but are rights that are capable of being inherited. For our purposes, the reference to a particular property right known as an easement is a good example. We will cover easements in more detail in Chapter 8 but will introduce them as an interest in land now as it will help to illustrate many of the concepts that we are covering in these initial chapters.

Key definition: Easement

A type of right that one landowner has over another landowner's land. A common example would be a right of way.

The legal right to walk across somebody else's land creates a right in relation to that land. It is not a tangible object (although there might be physical signs of the right – a pathway for example), but it nevertheless creates an interest in relation to the land that can be passed on to third parties. An easement is therefore a type of incorporeal hereditament and falls within the statutory definition of 'land'.

On-the-spot question

 Does a house come within the definition of 'land' as set out in s.205(1)(ix) of the Law of Property Act 1925? What about items within the house? Would a picture hanging on the wall become 'land'?

PROPRIETARY AND PERSONAL RIGHTS

If we develop the idea of land being a combination of both physical objects and intangible rights we can begin to understand that in relation to land some rights relate to (or attach to) land itself and others may be relevant only insofar as they relate to the individuals who have created them.

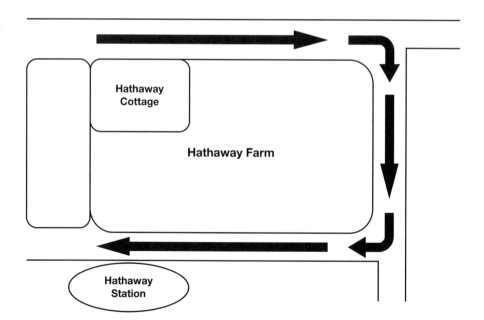

Figure 2.1 An example of how rights and interests in land might be created

Imagine, for example, that some years ago the owners of Hathaway Farm, in Figure 2.1, sold a cottage on their land to a third party. The current owners of Hathaway Cottage both travel to work by train and each morning have to follow the direction of the arrows, walking along the public highway that surrounds Hathaway Farm to get to the station.

A far quicker way for the owners of Hathaway Cottage to get to the station would be to take a short cut across Hathaway Farm. However, Hathaway Farm is private property and to do so would be a trespass on the land.

It is entirely possible that the owners of Hathaway Farm might be prepared to give their neighbours permission to walk across their land to get to the station. This permission could be given quite informally and by way of an oral agreement. This would create a personal right as between the owners of Hathaway Cottage and Hathaway Farm. You should, hopefully, instinctively recognise that this would not give the owners of Hathaway Cottage rights in relation to the land that forms Hathaway Farm. Instead, it is a personal permission that has been given that prevents their use of the shortcut from becoming a trespass. This permission could be revoked at any time and is given only to the owners for the time being of the cottage. Should the owners of Hathaway Farm change their minds, or the owners of Hathaway Cottage sell their property, then the permission would cease to have any effect.

On-the-spot question

 If the owners of Hathaway Farm, having made this informal arrangement with the owners of Hathaway Cottage, then decided to sell the farm do you think that the arrangement would have to be honoured by the new owners of the farm?

There would be an alternative way of giving the owners of Hathaway Cottage the right to cross over the land belonging to the farm. The owners of the farm could grant the owners of the cottage a formal right of way over their land. Provided the necessary formalities are met (and we will look at these later in the chapter), a right in relation to the land itself could be created. This would be an easement, capable of existing as a proprietary right, in other words a right in relation to land. This right, though intangible, is a valuable property right and attaches to the land itself. As a consequence, if Hathaway Farm was sold, the buyers, on the face of it, would purchase subject to the right of way over the land. Equally, if the owners of Hathaway Cottage were to sell, then their buyers would obtain the benefit of the right of way.

THE LEGAL ESTATE IN LAND

It is hopefully becoming apparent that a study of land law requires an understanding of people's rights in relation to land. It is hopefully also becoming clear that multiple rights can exist in relation to the same physical piece of land. The owners of Hathaway Farm have rights in relation to their property as owners. However, if a formal right of way is granted over Hathaway Farm for the benefit of their neighbours then those neighbours also have rights as a consequence of the easement.

If we start to think about land law as being about a hierarchy of rights then we would probably place ownership of land at the top. At this point we need to think about what it is that is actually 'owned'.

While a detailed history of the development of land law is outside the scope of this book it helps to understand the modern meaning of land 'ownership' to be aware of its roots. Its origins lie in the Norman Conquest of 1066 when William took control of all land in England and allowed those loyal to him possession of land in return for services to the King. Those servants of the Crown who were given rights to possess land did not own the land itself but were given 'tenure', a means by which they were allowed to hold and manage the land. The landholders in turn gave rights to others to possess and work the land and so a pyramid of landholding and possession developed at the top of which remained the King. The implications of this system were that no one other than the King actually 'owned' land. Instead, what they owned was an interest in the land that allowed them rights of possession for as long as they continued to fulfil their obligations to their superior.

Despite the passage of hundreds of years and the introduction and development of new systems of land ownership it is still the case that when we talk about owning a house we do not, in fact, own the physical land itself. What we own instead is an estate in the land. This stems from the fact that technically all land is still owned by the Crown and what we have, therefore, is a particular type of interest in the land that allows us to treat it as though it were our own.

Key definition: Estate

A right to possess land that is qualified by time.

The Law of Property Act 1925 recognises two legal estates in land. The first is the freehold and the second the leasehold. These terms will hopefully already be recognisable to you and the leasehold estate will be covered in more detail in Chapter 6. The freehold estate is referred to by the Law of Property Act 1925 as 'an estate in fee simple absolute in possession'. This, more detailed, term reflects the fact that what is owned is technically an interest in the land, but that this interest is indefinite, allowing the owner of the interest to dispose of it or leave it to someone else on death. The right is without limitation (absolute) and allows immediate enjoyment of the land (in possession) and so in many respects can be thought of as the most superior of interests in land. The leasehold estate, on the other hand, is referred to by the Law of Property Act 1925 as a 'term of years absolute' and is distinguished from the freehold by virtue of the fact that it is time limited. While under a lease you have ownership rights, these rights will disappear when the lease comes to an end.

On-the-spot question

 What do you think would happen to the freehold estate in land if the owner of that interest were to die and there was no one to inherit it?

The estate in land can therefore be distinguished from other interests that might be created and is more closely linked to the idea of 'ownership'. If I were to buy a house with the aid of a mortgage and my lender used my house as security for the loan then I will own the freehold estate in the property and my lender will take an interest in it. The interest that they acquire provides them with valuable property rights (which will be examined in more detail in Chapter 10), but this does not allow them the same rights that I have as a consequence of ownership of the freehold estate.

BOUNDARIES OF LAND OWNERSHIP

It is worth, at this point, briefly looking at issues relating to the extent of what is owned as a consequence of a freehold or leasehold estate. If we go back to the definition of land in the Law of Property Act 1925 there is an indication that land includes not just the surface of the earth but potentially also the subsoil beneath the ground and the air above the ground. Many land law textbooks will refer the reader to the principle 'he who owns the land owns everything up to the sky and down to the depths' (known as the *Accursius* principle). In modern life there are restrictions, both legal and practical, on what is actually owned. For example, statute has excluded ownership of coal and gas below the surface (by virtue of the Coal Industry Act 1994 and the Gas Act 1986), and has also intervened to prevent claims of trespass against aircraft flying overhead (see the Civil Aviation Act 1982).

The extent to which land is owned in terms of the horizontal division will depend on how the ownership of the land is demonstrated. Over the course of the next two chapters you will be introduced to two systems of land ownership, registered and unregistered. The documents that are used to demonstrate ownership of land under these two systems will ordinarily define the limits of what is owned. You should note, however, that boundaries are often identified in general terms only. There are often physical features that help to define these general boundaries; fences, walls, hedges and so on but these will not necessarily reflect the true *legal* boundaries of ownership. Often, owners of land are themselves not aware of the precise legal boundaries and conveyancing practice will ordinarily proceed satisfactorily on the basis that all boundaries are general only.

TRANSFERRING OWNERSHIP IN PROPERTY – INTRODUCTION TO CONVEYANCING PRACTICE

It might be helpful at this point to consider the basics of the process of transferring ownership in property. This is known as 'conveyancing'. While the practical steps that a lawyer will take in selling or buying real property is usually studied at postgraduate level, it is often helpful for students to appreciate some of the more important aspects in order to understand some of the land law concepts that we will introduce.

In its simplest form the conveyancing process has three stages and two key events that take place. The first key event is the exchange of contracts relating to the sale and purchase. It is at this point that the seller and buyer become bound to proceed with the transaction. Prior to exchange, either of the parties are at liberty to withdraw but exchange of contracts is perhaps best described as the 'point of no return', or at least if either of the parties do withdraw they will be in breach of their contract and the innocent party will be entitled to remedies. Importantly, though, this is not the point at which the parties involved actually move. From a lawyer's perspective, arguably, exchange of contracts is the most important part of the transaction but from a client's perspective they are aiming for the second key event which is called 'completion'. It is at this point that the bulk of the purchase monies are paid and the keys are handed over. From a legal perspective the document that will give effect to the transfer of ownership is dated or 'completed'.

Around the two key events of exchange of contracts and completion the solicitors involved will carry out a number of procedural tasks. Some of the more important tasks carried out on behalf of a buyer are included in Figure 2.2.

There are strict statutory requirements for the creation of a contract for the sale of land and the transfer deed, and these are summarised in Figure 2.3.

Pre-Contract Stage

- Receive and check the draft contract
- Check the seller's capacity to sell
- Check whether there are any other rights or interests affecting the land to be purchased
- Review any mortgage offer
- Arrange for signature of the contract and receipt of deposit

Post-Contract Stage

- Draft the legal transfer, (the document which gives effect to the sale and purchase)
- Make final checks in relation to the seller's ownership and ability to sell
- Request mortgage monies in readiness for completion

Post-Completion Stage

- Deal with payment of any stamp duty land tax
- Arrange for the transfer of ownership from seller to buyer to be registered at the Land Registry

Figure 2.2 The basic steps of the conveyancing process

Exchange of Contracts

- Contract must comply with s.2 Law of Property (Miscellaneous Provisions) Act 1989
  - Must be in writing
  - Must contain all agreed terms
  - Must be signed by all the parties to it

Completion

- Document used to transfer ownership must be in the form of a deed under s.52 Law of Property Act 1925
- s.2 Law of Property (Miscellaneous Provisions) Act 1989 set out requirements for a deed
  - Must state on its face that it is a deed
  - Must be executed as a deed
  - Must be delivered

Figure 2.3 Statutory requirements for the creation of a contact for the sale of land and transfer deed

Failure to comply with the requirements for a valid contract may result in the contract being treated as void. Failure to comply with the requirements for the use of a deed on completion will mean that the legal estate has not been transferred. For this reason it is vital that the formalities are followed.

Fixtures and chattels

If we have established that the term land comprises more than just the surface of the earth but will include buildings on the land, then what is the situation with items that are brought onto the land or introduced into the building? The topic of fixtures and chattels is often covered in the early stages of a land law module and has a particular relevance when considered in the context of modern house sales and purchases.

Key definitions

Fixture: an object that is treated as though it has become part of the land and has lost its individual characteristics.

Chattel: an object that retains its individual characteristics and remains a piece of personal property not attached to the land.

The importance of the distinction between items that are fixtures and chattels becomes most obvious when you consider the sale and purchase of a house. Items that are classified as fixtures and therefore form part of the land will, in the ordinary course of events, be automatically transferred along with the house on any sale. Chattels, on the other hand, remain the property of the seller and can be removed by them at any point prior to completion of the sale taking place. It has often been the source of irritation to buyers to move into their new house on the date of completion only to find that the house has been stripped bare of light bulbs and fittings. Of even more concern might be the buyer who made a financial offer based on the expectation of inclusion of valuable items that are then removed by the seller when they move out.

The tests that are used to determine whether items are fixtures or chattels come from the case of *Holland v Hodgson* [1872] LR 7 CP 328. In deciding the classification of an object the degree of annexation and the purpose of annexation must be considered.

KEY CASE ANALYSIS: *Holland v Hodgson* **[1872] LR 7 CP 328**

Background

Spinning looms were nailed to the floor of a mill. The owner of the mill had mortgaged the property and was in default on the loan. The lender had repossessed the mill and the court had to decide whether the looms were fixtures (and therefore passed to the lender as part of the land) or chattels.

Decision

The tests to apply were (a) the degree of annexation of the object to the land and (b) the object or purpose of the annexation. In this case the looms were held to be fixtures as a consequence of their attachment to the building.

The application of the tests to determine whether an object is a fixture or a fitting will depend on the circumstances in each case. The modern application of the tests seems to place emphasis on the second test, that of purpose. In the case of *Elitestone v Morris* [1997] 1 WLR 687, for example, bungalows that rested by their own weight on concrete pillars were held to be fixtures, part and parcel of the land itself. While the degree of annexation was low, the fact that to remove the bungalows would have meant demolishing them persuaded the court that they could not be treated as chattels.

A useful and modern examination of everyday household objects is contained in the case of *Botham v TSB* (1997) 73 P&CR D1, a case that also related to a repossessed property.

On-the-spot question

You act for a client who, on moving into her new house, has noticed that several items have been removed including a large, American style free-standing fridge freezer from the kitchen and wardrobes that had been built in to the alcoves of the main bedroom. In removing the wardrobes significant damage has been caused. What advice would you offer to the client?

Many of the problems associated with determining whether items are fixtures or chattels are resolved in modern conveyancing practice where a lengthy checklist of items included in the sale is produced by sellers as part of the contractual documentation.

You are hopefully now beginning to recognise that a study of land law involves the consideration of rights and interests in relation to land. We have looked at some of those interests already. So, ownership of an estate in land is clearly a superior interest as close to absolute ownership as you can get. Sitting alongside are a range of lesser interests that are nevertheless capable of attaching to the land itself (*proprietary* interests). Now we need to introduce a new dimension: the fact that rights and interests in land can be classified as being either legal or equitable.

LEGAL AND EQUITABLE INTERESTS IN LAND

As students of law you will be introduced to the body of rules that were developed by the Court of Chancery to offer flexibility and fairness as an alternative to the more rigid and inflexible rules of the common law courts. This body of rules became known as equity. While a detailed discussion of the development and importance of equity is outside the scope of this book (but is introduced in *Beginning Equity*), these rules play a very important part in the understanding of land law.

As you work through this book you will come to realise that interests in land are capable of existing either as legal interests or as equitable interests. Some interests, the restrictive covenant for example, are direct creations of equity. Other interests, expressly granted easements for example, can exist as legal interests but only where the appropriate formalities for their creation are followed. Where the formalities are not followed, equity will often step in to prevent the creation of an interest failing altogether by recognising it as an equitable interest instead.

Key definition: Restrictive covenant

A promise *not* to do something in relation to land. Perhaps not to build on land or not to use the land other than as a private dwellinghouse.

We will see that generally the creation of legal interests requires compliance with formalities, whereas the creation of equitable interests often comes about quite informally.

This in turn means that equitable interests are often more vulnerable than legal interests and need to be protected in order to ensure that they are binding on third parties.

The development of the trust

Many textbooks describe the trust as the most important creation of the Court of Chancery. It also has an important function in the operation of land law. Where a trust exists in relation to land it creates a separation of legal and beneficial (equitable) ownership. Imagine, for example, that a husband and wife purchase a property together, both contributing to the costs of the acquisition, but the deed of transfer that is entered into transfers ownership of the legal estate into the husband's name only. For a variety of reasons it will be important that there is some recognition of the wife's interest. The couple may well want to recognise this formally, so that were the husband to die, for example, the wife would remain entitled to the family home. Equity would also recognise the wife's beneficial interest as a consequence of her financial contributions to the purchase. Remember equity acts to introduce fairness and would therefore recognise that while not a legal owner of the property the wife's contributions mean that she must have an interest that is recognised.

In the very simple example in Figure 2.4 the result is that the husband owns the legal interest in the property and the husband and wife both also have an equitable interest.

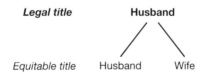

Figure 2.4 The separation of legal and beneficial ownership

Common law recognises the ownership of the legal estate but equity recognises beneficial interests as being the more important.

A trust can arise in any number of situations. As we saw earlier in the chapter, if the formal requirements of a deed are not followed when drafting a transfer on the sale of land then the completed transfer will not effectively transfer the legal estate. If this occurs the legal estate will remain with the seller but the seller will then hold that legal estate on trust for the benefit of the buyer who will hold an equitable interest until such time as the legal estate is properly transferred.

We will introduce in Chapter 5 the ways in which the equitable ownership can be held by beneficial owners. However, at this point it is important to recognise that this equitable interest is an interest in relation to land and one that, in certain circumstances, can be binding on third parties.

SUMMARY

- The legal definition of land is contained in s.205(1)(ix) of the Law of Property Act 1925 and combines the tangible, physical aspects of land with intangible rights and interests that relate to the land.
- When rights are created they can be personal or proprietary. Proprietary rights attach to the land itself so that when the land is sold the rights are transferred together with the land.
- Land 'ownership' in legal terms relates to ownership of an 'estate' in land, rather than the land itself. There are two legal estates in land: the freehold and the leasehold.
- Interests in land can be legal or equitable and the ways in which interests are created will differ depending on the nature of the interest and the formalities required.

FURTHER READING

Dixon, M., *Modern Land Law*, 9th edn (Routledge, 2014) – the introduction to this textbook contains a very useful overview.

Gray, K. and Gray, S. F., *Elements of Land Law*, 7th edn (OUP, 2011) – the 'Fundamental Concepts' section of this book provides a comprehensive discussion of how land law has developed.

Koo, A. K. C., 'Proving Property Boundaries' (2013) *The Conveyancer and Property Lawyer 5* – an interesting article that looks at the challenges faced by courts in settling boundary disputes.

Land Registry website: www.landregistry.gov.uk/public/boundaries – a basic introduction to boundaries.

Ramjohn, M., *Beginning Equity and Trusts*, 1st edn (Routledge, 2013) – contains a more detailed introduction to equity and trusts.

Chapter 3
An introduction to registered land

LEARNING OBJECTIVES

After reading this chapter, you should be able to:

- explain why and how the system of registered land has developed and its importance in the study of land law;
- identify how title to registered land is demonstrated;
- compare and contrast the different ways in which interests are protected in registered land;
- appreciate the nature and significance of overriding interests.

INTRODUCTION

By now you are beginning to recognise that a study of land law involves an understanding of the nature of rights and interests that can exist in relation to land. In the last chapter you were introduced to the concept of the 'estate' in land and should now appreciate that there are two legal estates that are capable of existing: the freehold and leasehold.

In this chapter we will review how ownership of the legal estate is demonstrated, what is meant by 'title' to land and how rights and interests in relation to land are protected. This chapter will focus on the concepts in so far as they relate to registered land. Chapter 4 will make comparisons with the system of unregistered land. You will also begin to recognise that there are sometimes anomalies in relation to the law that need to be understood in order to develop a thorough and deeper understanding of land law.

THE MEANING OF 'TITLE' TO LAND

Imagine that you are buying a new house and have instructed solicitors to act on your behalf. One of the most important issues that you will want to be checked is that the person who is selling you the house is actually the owner and that they are able and have authority to sell the house to you. It follows that there has to be a system in place for owners of property to be able to demonstrate their ownership and ability to sell. They do this by demonstrating their 'title' to the property.

Key definition: Title

Ownership of an estate in land and the property rights related to that land. The term is often also used by lawyers to describe the evidence of ownership in land.

Alongside a demonstration of ownership buyers will also want to check those rights and interests in relation to land that will continue to bind them following their purchase. So, for example, a buyer would want to know if neighbours were exercising rights of way over the back garden of the property they were intending to purchase. They would want to check the nature of those rights and whether they were obliged to allow their neighbours to continue to exercise them once they had completed their purchase and moved in.

On-the-spot question

 If you were in the process of buying a house what issues do you think would be of concern to you? Can you think of any rights that others might have in relation to the house that would potentially cause you concern?

So, in demonstrating title to land an owner is producing evidence of their ownership of an estate in the land and also those rights and interests that affect the land. The ways in which they will do this will depend on whether the title is registered or unregistered.

THE DEVELOPMENT OF A SYSTEM OF LAND REGISTRATION

As you will discover in Chapter 4 it used to be the case that land and ownership of land could only be identified through the deeds and documents created to transfer title and create interests in relation to that land. It was recognised that this system was unwieldy and potentially open to abuse and over a number of years a system of limited registration of land was developed. The sweeping legislation of 1925 was designed to create a universal system of registration of title to land in England and Wales. You have already been introduced to the Law of Property Act 1925 and the Land Registration Act of the same year introduced the means by which registration would take place.

The system of land registration was founded on three principles; the mirror principle, the curtain principle and the insurance principle which are still relevant to a study of registered land today (see Figure 3.1).

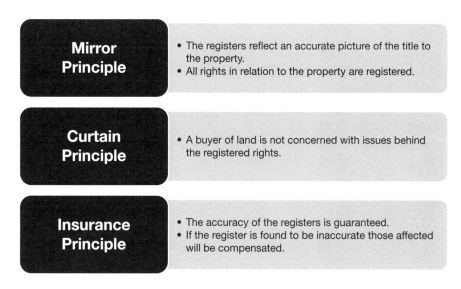

Figure 3.1 The three principles of land registration

The three principles underline the fact that the aim of the 1925 legislation was to create a simplified and transparent means by which title to land could be recorded and evidenced. As a buyer you are entitled to rely on the title registers as accurate and, with limited exceptions, as recording all of the interests in land to which any sale is made subject.

THE REGISTERS OF TITLE

Land registration is administered by the Land Registry, a government department that maintains the land register. There are currently more than 23 million titles registered at the Land Registry and the public are entitled to obtain copies of the registers to check ownership of land and interests in relation to the land. Since 2000 the Land Registry also records the prices paid for property in England and Wales.

When you apply to see evidence of registered title you are provided with copies of the entries on the appropriate register and, if requested, a title plan indicating the general boundaries of the property. A sample register of title, reproduced with the kind permission of Land Registry, is included in this chapter by way of example.

The registers are split into three parts; property register, proprietorship register and charges register. Figure 3.2 gives you an indication of the information that can be found in each register.

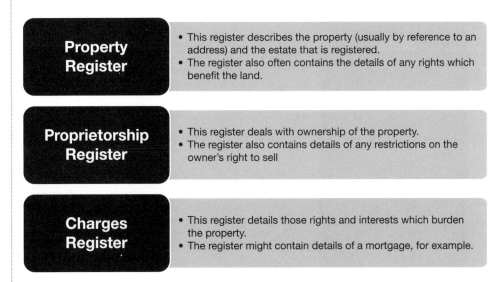

Property Register
- This register describes the property (usually by reference to an address) and the estate that is registered.
- The register also often contains the details of any rights which benefit the land.

Proprietorship Register
- This register deals with ownership of the property.
- The register also contains details of any restrictions on the owner's right to sell

Charges Register
- This register details those rights and interests which burden the property.
- The register might contain details of a mortgage, for example.

Figure 3.2 The registers that make up a registered title

During the house buying and selling process the buyer's solicitor will check the registers of title (see Figure 3.3) to ensure that the person purporting to sell is capable of transferring title to the buyer and to report on and investigate any registered interests that might affect the seller's ability to sell and the buyer's subsequent enjoyment of the property.

On-the-spot question

Read through the sample title register and see whether you can spot the following:

- the legal estate that is registered;
- the names of the owners of the property;
- whether the property is mortgaged and, if so, to whom;
- the price that was paid for the property by the current owners.

Land Registry

Official copy of register of title	Title number CS72510	Edition date 11.04.2007

- This official copy shows the entries in the register of title on 23 July 2007 at 11:39:46.
- This date must be quoted as the "search from date" in any official search application based on this copy.
- The date at the beginning of an entry is the date on which the entry was made in the register.
- Issued on 23 July 2007.
- Under s.67 of the Land Registration Act 2002, this copy is admissible in evidence to the same extent as the original.
- For information about the register of title see Land Registry website www.landregistry.gov.uk or Land Registry Public Guide 1 – *A guide to the information we keep and how you can obtain it.*
- This title is dealt with by Land Registry Maradon office.

A: Property register
The register describes the registered estate comprised in the title.

CORNSHIRE : MARADON

1. (19.12.1989) The Freehold land shown edged with red on the plan of the above title filed at Land Registry and being 13 Augustine Way, Kerwick (PL14 3JP).

2. (19.12.1989) The land has the benefit of a right of way on foot only over the passageway at the rear leading into Monk's Mead.

3. (03.12.2003) The exact line of the boundary of the land in this title (between the points A – B in blue on the title plan) is determined under section 60 of the Land Registration Act 2002 as shown on the plan lodged with the application to determine the boundary dated 3 December 2003.

    Note: Plan filed.

B: Proprietorship register
This register specifies the class of title and identifies the owner. It contains any entries that affect the right of disposal.

Title absolute

1. (10.07.2000) PROPRIETOR: PAUL JOHN DAWKINS and ANGELA MARY DAWKINS both of 28 Nelson Way, Kerwick, Maradon, Cornshire PL14 5PQ and of pjdawkins@ail.com.

2. (10.07.2000) The price stated to have been paid on 2 June 2000 was £78,000.

Page 1 of 2

Figure 3.3 A sample register of title, reproduced with the kind permission of Land Registry

Title Number CS72510]

3. (10.07.2000) RESTRICTION: No disposition by a sole proprietor of the
    registered estate (except a trust corporation) under which capital money
    arises is to be registered unless authorised by the Court.

4. (05.10.2002) Caution in favour of Mary Gertrude Shelley of 18 Cambourne
    Street, Kerwick, Maradon, Cornshire PL14 7AR and of Messrs Swan & Co of 25
    Trevisick Street, Kerwick, Maradon, Cornshire PL14 6RE.

5. (28.11.2003) RESTRICTION: No disposition of the registered estate by the
    proprietor of the registered estate is to be registered without a written
    consent signed by the proprietor for the time being of the Charge dated 12
    November 2003 in favour of Fast and Furious Building Society referred to in
    the Charges register.

C: Charges register

This register contains any charges and other matters that affect the registered
estate.

1. (19.12.1989) The passageway at the side is included in the title is subject to
    rights of way on foot only.

2. (10.07.2000) A Transfer of the land in this title dated 2 June 2000 made
    between (1) John Charles Brown and (2) Paul John Dawkins and Angela Mary
    Dawkins contains restrictive covenants.

    NOTE: Original filed.

3. (01.08.2002) REGISTERED CHARGE dated 15 July 2002 to secure the moneys
    including the further advances therein mentioned.

4. (01.08.2002) Proprietor: WEYFORD BUILDING SOCIETY of Society House, The
    Avenue, Weyford, Cornshire CN12 4BD.

5. (28.11.2003) REGISTERED CHARGE dated 12 November 2003.

6. (28.11.2003) Proprietor: FAST AND FURIOUS BUILDING SOCIETY of Fast Plaza, The
    Quadrangle, Weyford, Cornshire CN14 3NW.

7. (03.12.2003) The parts of the land affected thereby are subject to the leases
    set out in the schedule of leases hereto.

Schedule of notices of leases

1.	*Registration date and Plan ref.*	*Property description*	*Date of lease and Term*	*Lessee's Title*
	03.12.2003	13 Augustine Way, Kerwick	12.11.2003 999 years from 10.10.2003	CS385372

End of register

Figure 3.3 *continued*

Once the principles and purpose of land registration are understood the next question is: *what* rights and interests need to be recorded and *how* are they recorded on the registers? In order to answer that question we need to consider the Land Registration Act 2002.

MODERN LAND REGISTRATION AND THE LAND REGISTRATION ACT 2002

The Land Registration Act 2002 made significant changes to the ways in which land and interests in land are registered. Its aim was to try to make the registers of title a more accurate reflection of the rights and interests that affect a registered estate and to make clearer provision as to how rights in registered land are protected and how they work in relation to each other. It has also facilitated a push towards increased registration of land and as a consequence the amount of unregistered title in England and Wales is diminishing.

Registration of the legal estate

As we saw in Chapter 2 there are only two estates in land capable of existing as legal estates. They are the freehold and leasehold. Both of these estates are capable of being registered with their own titles (referred to as *substantive* registration). There are only three other interests in land that are capable of being registered with independent titles. These are a rentcharge, a franchise and a profit à prendre. The suggested further reading will give you some resources that will provide more detailed explanations about these interests.

The Land Registration Act 2002 extended the 'triggers' for first registration of land, in other words the dealings with the freehold and leasehold estates that would require title to be registered for the first time. As a consequence if you acquire an unregistered title to freehold land following a purchase you will be required to register the land on completion of that purchase. In addition if you acquire the land as a consequence of a gift or inheritance you will also need to register your title. There does not necessarily even need to be a transfer of legal title as if you decide to mortgage land already owned then this will also potentially trigger a requirement for registration. In relation to the leasehold estate you will have to register any new lease granted for a term of seven years or more as well as any transfer of an existing lease where there is more than seven years of the term left to run.

Key definition: Term

In relation to leaseholds this means the period for which a lease is granted.

It is not even necessary now to wait for one of these trigger events to occur. You are entitled to voluntarily register your title with the Land Registry on payment of a fee. You might decide to do this, for example, prior to a sale of land if the unregistered title is particularly complicated and you want to facilitate a smooth conveyancing process.

These triggers and opportunities for first registration are designed to increase the amount of registered land in England and Wales. There are consequences, where there is a requirement for registration, if this does not take place within the timescales set out. Failure to register a transfer of unregistered land within two months of completion of the purchase, for example, will result in the title reverting to the seller (who then holds the legal estate on trust for the buyer).

Once a title is registered, subsequent transfers of the registered estate will also require registration under s.27(1) of the Land Registration Act 2002 in order to ensure that the disposal has legal effect. Failure to register means that legal title to the property has not been transferred. This may come as a surprise to buyers who assume that once they have handed over the purchase monies they own the property. In fact true ownership of a legal title only occurs once registration has taken place.

On-the-spot question

 A couple who purchased an unregistered title to a freehold house in 1995 are shocked to discover when they come to sell the house that they have never been registered as proprietors. Do they have any title to the house they are trying to sell?

Registration of subsidiary interests

As we have seen, a buyer of land will be interested to check not only that the seller is the owner of a legal estate but also those interests or rights in relation to the land that will continue to bind the buyer after completion of their purchase. These subsidiary interests usually need protecting by registration themselves, although they are not registered with their own title but sit on the registers of title relating to the estate that they affect. There are a number of examples of subsidiary interest in the sample register of title in this chapter. Each numbered point on the register is called an 'entry' and we will highlight some of the important ones in this section.

It is important to remember that the interests that are registered are *proprietary* in nature, in other words they are interests that relate to the land rather than the individuals who have created them. The principles of land registration mean that once registered these rights are capable of binding third parties who acquire the land.

The way in which the interests are registered depends on the nature of the interest itself. Arguably in practical terms all we are really concerned with is the fact of registration itself but it is important to understand why and how different interests are protected. Interests capable of being registered will fall into one of two categories: registrable interests under s.27 of the Land Registration Act 2002 or third party interests protected by the registration of a notice or restriction. Those interests that are treated as *registrable* interests under s.27(2) of the Land Registration Act 2002 include the grant of a lease with more than seven years left to run from the date of the grant (see Entry 7 of the Charges Register and the Schedule of Leases in the sample register), legal easements (see Entry 1 of the Charges Register in the sample register) and legal charges, (usually protecting a mortgage – see Entries 3 to 6 of the Charges Register of the sample register). These interests belong to a narrow category of interests that are all capable of existing as legal interests under the provisions of s.1(2) of the Law of Property Act 1925.

> ## Key definition: Registrable interest
>
> An interest in land that is required to be protected by registration.

Failure to register these interests means that they will not have any legal effect. This does not necessarily mean that they are void but may be treated as equitable interests only which, as we will see shortly, themselves require protection in order to be binding on third parties. If they are registered, however, then they will automatically bind any buyer of the legal estate.

Any interest in land that is not capable of existing as a legal interest under s.1(2) of the Law of Property Act 1925 will, instead, take effect as an equitable interest. These rights are classified by the Land Registration Act 2002 as third party interests. They are protected by registration of a notice or restriction in the registers of title to the estate that they affect. There are a number of interests that are capable of being protected by the registration of a notice but the most common would include restrictive covenants, equitable easements and estate contracts. An example of a notice protecting a restrictive covenant is contained at Entry 2 of the Charges Register of the sample register, but note that in itself this entry does not give details of the nature of the covenants but requires an application to the Land Registry for a copy of the transfer that contains them.

Key definition: Notice

An entry made in the title registers in respect of the burden of an interest that affects a registered estate.

Key definition: Restriction

An entry made in the title registers that prevents or restricts the registration of a disposal of the registered estate.

The registration of a notice is usually found in the Charges Register and its purpose is to give notice to prospective buyers of the existence of the interest in relation to the land.

As an alternative to the notice a restriction might be registered. As the term suggests a restriction is designed to prevent a disposal of the land without the restriction first being complied with. A lender might register a restriction, for example, to alert prospective buyers to the existence of a legal charge and to prevent the owners selling the land without first paying the debt due to the lender. Restrictions are usually contained within the Proprietorship Register and Entry 5 of the Proprietorship Register of the sample register provides an example.

THE PRIORITY OF INTERESTS IN REGISTERED LAND

You will now understand that in relation to one piece of registered land there may be a number of interests that are capable of binding buyers of the land and that have to be protected in some way by registration in order to take effect. The Land Registration Act 2002 talks about protected interests having 'priority' over other interests. In s.29 of the Act it states that where a registered estate in land is sold for valuable consideration and the sale triggers a registration of the title then that registration will take effect subject to any interest that has been protected. However, any interest that is not protected will be postponed – in other words it will *not* be binding on the new purchaser.

Key definition: Valuable consideration

A payment which is of economic value, usually money. Note that the Land Registration Act specifically excludes from this definition gifts in consideration of marriage or nominal consideration in money.

---

s.29(2) of the Land Registration Act 2002 sets out those interests whose priority is protected. These include registered charges or interests that are the subject of a notice in the title registers. It follows, therefore, that interests in registered land that have been protected by registration will be binding on purchasers for valuable consideration of the registered estate. The various entries contained within our sample register will, therefore, all be capable of binding buyers of the legal estate.

By way of a further example, think again about the nature of an easement as a right in land. Easements are capable of existing as legal interests in land by virtue of s.1(2) of the Law of Property Act 1925. As such, in order to take effect as a legal interest they are required to be registered, (they are a *registrable* interest). Failure to register means that they cannot take effect in law but they are still capable of existing as equitable interests. As an equitable interest an easement would still need to be protected by the registration of a notice in order to be binding on third parties. It follows then, applying s.29 of the Land Registration Act 2002 that if the easement has not been registered either as a legal interest or by way of notice protecting an equitable interest it will not be binding on buyers of the land because it will have lost its priority.

It is perhaps worth noting that s.29 refers specifically to buyers who have paid for their purchase, i.e. have given valuable consideration. The same does not apply, for example, to people who may acquire property as a consequence of a gift. A transfer through a gift will still prompt a registration of the estate but the new registered owner will not have priority over any interest created prior to the gift – whether it has been registered or not.

THE ANOMALY OF OVERRIDING INTERESTS

You should now appreciate the principles of land registration and the ways in which interests in land can be protected. The idea of the registers of title being a transparent means of recording all interests relating to a piece of land should be quite straightforward.

However, as is often the case there are exceptions to the rules and the category of interests known as 'overriding interests' are, unfortunately, one of those. The mirror principle, explained earlier in this chapter, suggests that all rights in relation to land are registered. In fact, there is a category of interests in relation to registered land that do not require registration but are nevertheless binding on buyers of the land. Perhaps even more crucially, they are binding whether or not the buyer knows about them. These interests are known as overriding interests.

Key definition: Overriding interest

An interest to which a registered title is subject notwithstanding the fact that the interest does not appear on the registers of title.

This would, of course, seem to fly in the face of everything we had said about registered land and the aim to have a system of registration that is simple and transparent. The Land Registration Act 2002 cut down the number of interests that are capable of existing as overriding interests but, unfortunately, it did not get rid of this category of interest altogether. It might be helpful as a starting point to think about the reasons why this category of interest continues to exist by reference to an example.

Imagine that an individual purchases a property, registers themselves as owner and occupies the property as their home. Some time later they meet someone and eventually their partner decides to move in with them. For a number of years they live together and both contribute towards payment of the mortgage. Perhaps the partner also invests their own money in the development and improvement of the property over the years. Eventually the relationship breaks down and the couple decide to separate and sell the house. Despite the financial contributions that the partner has made over the years they have never been registered on the title to the property and therefore have no legal estate. When it comes to a sale the registers of title would indicate only the original purchaser as legal title owner and on the face of it the partner has no rights at all. However, equity recognises the rights that the partner may have acquired as an interest in the land and the Land Registration Act 2002 will protect these in some circumstances as overriding interests. This might arise even though the partner may not themselves initially be aware of this interest.

KEY CASE ANALYSIS: *Williams & Glyns Bank Ltd v Boland* **[1981] AC 487**

Background

Mr Boland owned the legal title to a house in his sole name although his wife had made substantial contributions towards the purchase price and mortgage payments. He subsequently borrowed money, using the house as security and when he defaulted on his repayments the bank wanted to take possession of the house and sell it to recover the debt.

Decision

The House of Lords found that Mr Boland's wife had a trust interest that was capable of being an overriding interest and so was binding on the bank.

While *Williams & Glyn's Bank v Boland* was decided before the Land Registration Act 2002, the interest of individuals in actual occupation of property is still recognised as an overriding interest by paragraph 2 of Schedule 3 of the Act and is one of the more important categories of overriding interest still capable of existing. Importantly, to acquire an overriding interest the person claiming the right must show that at the time of the disposition of the property they had an *interest* and were also in *actual occupation*. The interest must be a proprietary interest, in other words an interest in the land itself. The interest acquired through the example given above will be a beneficial interest under a trust and the decision in *Williams & Glyns Bank v Boland* confirms that this will be sufficient to acquire a proprietary interest. An occupier of property who is there as a consequence of a mere permission or licence on the other hand and who has not made direct or indirect contributions financially to the property is unlikely to be treated as having an interest in the land.

Whether or not an individual is in actual occupation is a question of fact. It has been held that physical presence is required (*Williams & Glyn's Bank v Boland*) and there must be some degree of permanence and continuity to the occupation, although brief interruptions in occupation have not precluded a claim for an overriding interest.

KEY CASE ANALYSIS: *Chhokar v Chhokar* **[1984] Fam Law 269**

Background

While his wife was in hospital having a baby, a husband who was the sole legal title owner of the family home sold the house. The wife returned from hospital to find that the locks had been changed.

Decision

The court held that the wife's temporary absence did not prevent her from being treated as though in actual occupation. There was clear evidence of her intention to return.

The Land Registration Act 2002 does include a limitation on the right to claim an overriding interest. If the occupation would not have been obvious on a reasonably careful inspection of the land at the time of the disposition and the buyer of the registered title does not have actual knowledge of the occupation then the buyer will buy free of the interest.

On-the-spot question

? A husband and wife purchased a house 10 years ago, each of them contributing towards the purchase price. Only the husband was registered as proprietor of the property. Their relationship broke down and the husband entered into negotiations to sell the house without informing his wife. While the wife was away visiting relatives abroad the husband completed the sale and vacated the property. What rights, if any, does the wife have?

The interests of those in actual occupation are just one example of interests that are capable of overriding registration. The Land Registration Act 2002 aimed to reduce the number of interests capable of existing as overriding interests but there are a number of interests that retain their status under the Act. They include all easements created before the coming into force of the Land Registration Act 2002 (the Act came into force on 13 October 2003) and easements created by implied grant or prescription after the coming into force of the Act. The creation of easements and their protection by registration will be picked up in more detail in Chapter 8. They also include short term legal leases for a term not exceeding seven years (remember that leases of seven years and over require substantive registration under the Act).

SUMMARY

- On a sale of land a seller will be required to demonstrate that they have good title to the property. In registered land this will involve producing the appropriate registers of title for the buyer to review.
- The registers of title will include details of the legal estate, the registered proprietor, notices protecting interests in relation to the land and any restrictions on the owners' ability to deal with the land.
- Registered interests are 'protected' and therefore binding on third parties.
- Overriding interests are a category of interests that are binding on buyers of land even if they have not been registered. They include the interests of individuals in actual occupation of the property.

FURTHER READING

Gray, K. and Gray, S. F., *Land Law*, 7th edn (Oxford, 2011) – this book will help you to understand the nature of rent charges and profits à prendre.

The Land Registry public guides: www.landregistry.gov.uk/public/guides – a useful source of basic information about the role of the Land Registry.

The Land Registration Act 2002: www.legislation.gov.uk/ukpga/2002/9/contents.

The Land Registry website: www.landregistry.gov.uk/public/our-terminology-explained – a useful online glossary of terms often used in land registration.

Warner-Reed, E., *Optimize Land Law*, 1st edn (Routledge, 2014) – this book has a useful summary of the principles of land registration and helps you to contextualise registered land in relation to other areas that you will study.

Chapter 4
Unregistered land

LEARNING OBJECTIVES

After reading this chapter, you should be able to:

- explain how title is demonstrated in relation to unregistered land;
- recognise the differences between the systems of registered and unregistered land;
- appreciate the importance of the legislation of 1925 and the changes that it made to the system of unregistered land;
- compare and contrast the different means by which interests in relation to unregistered land are protected today.

INTRODUCTION

Many land law textbooks take a chronological approach to the explanation of the two systems of demonstrating title to land. They will often start with the traditional way in which title was deduced and so will introduce unregistered title to land first of all. They will then look at how a system of land registration was introduced in England and Wales and will start to consider the system of registered land and make comparisons between the two.

In this book we introduce you to the system of registered land first of all. There are two reasons for this. The first is that the system of demonstrating title and interests in relation to land where title is registered is much more straightforward and enables you to reinforce your developing knowledge of estates and interests in land in a context that is generally easier to grasp. The second reason is that the vast majority of land in England and Wales is now registered and so the occasions when you will come across and be required to deal with unregistered title in legal practice are diminishing.

That said there are still areas of land that have not yet been registered. Often this occurs when land and property have been owned for long periods by the same people or organisations without any transactions in relation to it taking place. As a consequence, nothing has happened to trigger a registration of the title to that land. In those situations we still need to be aware of how title to unregistered land is demonstrated and how rights in relation to the land are protected. For that reason it remains important to introduce students to key concepts relating to unregistered title, which is the aim of this chapter.

DEMONSTRATING TITLE TO UNREGISTERED LAND

Historically, title to land was demonstrated through possession of that land. There was (and remains) no absolute ownership of land and so you demonstrated your ability to deal with and dispose of your land by the fact of your possession. Your rights to possess the land were evidenced by producing title deeds that recorded transmissions of title through to you.

Key definition: Title deeds

A collection of legal documents that together demonstrate title to unregistered land.

It remains the case that a buyer of an unregistered title will need to check the title deeds (usually through their solicitor) to ensure that the person purporting to sell has the capacity and is able to do this. In theory this would require the seller to produce all of the title deeds that they hold in relation to the property and build up a chain of possession at the top of which would be the seller. This would potentially mean producing a multitude of documents forming that chain potentially stretching back many years (bear in mind that they could include transfers of title, mortgages, leases, grants of easements and so on). From a buyer's point a view it also potentially creates the huge task of having to go through each and every document of title to check that the chain is not broken and to ensure that there are no issues relating to the documents that might cause them a problem.

Modern conveyancing practice aims to simplify the process of demonstrating title to unregistered land by requiring that a seller must produce title deeds going back a minimum of 15 years from the current title owner. The document that forms the start of the chain is called the 'root of title' and all dealings and dispositions of the land that have occurred since that document are required to be produced. Given my comment in the introduction that much unregistered land may have been owned by the same person for many years this will generally now mean that the quantity of documents that has to be produced has been greatly reduced. The seller's solicitor will produce a list of the documents to be provided in chronological order and will provide photocopies of the documents for the buyer's solicitor to review. This is called an 'epitome of title'.

On-the-spot question

? You act for a client who has held the unregistered title to farmland for over 40 years and who has now decided to sell. Since they acquired the title they have not made any dispositions of the land, have not mortgaged it or created any other interests. Which documents do you think will need to be produced in order to demonstrate your client's title?

From a buyer's perspective they (or more usually their solicitor) will have to read and analyse each of the title documents produced and check that the seller has acquired a title that they are able to dispose of to the buyer. Where there are gaps in the title or deficiencies in the documents that have been produced the buyer will have to raise enquiries of the seller and obtain satisfactory answers before proceeding with their purchase. Remember that after the sale of the unregistered title has completed there will be a requirement on the buyer to get their title registered. On application to the Land Registry the unregistered title will be scrutinised before a register is created. The Land Registry will not be concerned about raising their own enquiries of the buyer if they perceive there to be difficulties with the title produced and so it is important at an early stage to identify any potential problems.

INTERESTS IN RELATION TO UNREGISTERED TITLE

As with registered title it is, of course, important to check not only the seller's capacity to sell unregistered land but also to be aware of those rights and interests that might continue to bind a buyer after their purchase.

In the system of registered land we saw that, subject to the anomaly of overriding interests, a buyer is entitled to rely on the entries on the registers of title as conclusive evidence of those rights and interests that affect the property. The question of whether the rights, once registered, are legal or equitable is arguably not important. If they are registered then they are binding on buyers who acquire title to the land. This makes the process of checking third party rights much easier because they are recorded in one place. Unfortunately the position is not quite as straightforward in relation to unregistered land.

In unregistered land the distinction between legal and equitable rights becomes more important. The guiding principle traditionally is that legal rights are automatically binding on the world and equitable rights are subject to the doctrine of notice. This means that where a legal interest has been created in relation to unregistered land, an expressly granted legal easement perhaps, it is automatically binding on anyone who acquires the legal estate in the land. There is no requirement for registration or other protection – the nature of the interest as a *legal* interest in land is sufficient for it to be binding. If an equitable interest has been created, on the other hand, perhaps a trust interest of a third party in occupation of the land, then its ability to bind others is reliant on the doctrine of notice. The importance of the doctrine of notice was greatly reduced by the Land Charges Act 1925. The implications of this are set out below.

The doctrine of notice

The doctrine of notice provides that equitable interests will bind a buyer of land unless that person purchases the legal estate in good faith, for value and without notice of the existence of the equitable interest. We can therefore break the requirements down into four parts. First, the doctrine applies only to the purchaser of a legal estate or interest. These concepts should by now be familiar to you. Second, the purchaser must have acted in good faith. Land law textbooks often refer to the 'bona fide' purchaser as being someone who enters into the purchase in good conscience and with honest intention. Third, there is a requirement for valuable consideration so that someone inheriting or acquiring property as a consequence of a gift would be subject to any equitable interests affecting the land. Finally, the purchaser must have no notice of the equitable interest. In order to fully understand the meaning of the doctrine we need to understand what is meant by 'notice'. Figure 4.1 illustrates the three different types of notice that are relevant in relation to the purchase of unregistered land.

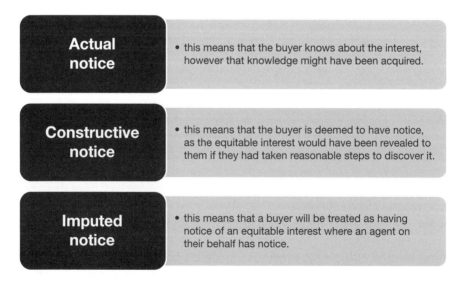

Figure 4.1 The three different types of notice that are relevant in relation to the purchase of unregistered land

On the basis that buyers will be subject to both interests that they actually knew about and also interests that they *should* have known about it follows that prudent buyers of land will always carry out investigations to discover whether there are interests, legal or equitable, that might be binding on them following purchase. In conveyancing practice these kinds of checks are fairly routine. A buyer's solicitor will examine the seller's unregistered title both to review their capacity to sell and to investigate whether any such rights are recorded. A previous conveyance of land might have included easements over the land or restrictive covenants in terms of the use of the land. On an inspection of land a prudent buyer will also check to see whether there is any evidence of third parties who may potentially have rights (perhaps another adult in occupation of the property who has not previously been disclosed to the buyer). The buyer's solicitors will also raise fairly standard enquiries of the seller prior to entering into contracts to check for such third party rights.

It is important to appreciate that imputed notice operates to fix on a buyer notice of any rights or interests of which their agent is aware. So, a buyer's solicitor is effectively acting as their agent and, as a result, if the solicitor becomes aware of an interest affecting the land then the buyer is deemed to have notice also. A good example of how imputed notice operates comes from the case of *Kingsnorth Finance Ltd v Tizard*.

KEY CASE ANALYSIS: *Kingsnorth Finance Co Ltd v Tizard* [1986] 1 WLR 783

Background

Mr Tizard purchased a house together with his wife. Both contributed financially towards the acquisition but only Mr Tizard owned the legal title. The relationship broke down and Mrs Tizard spent periods away from the matrimonial home but returned on a daily basis to look after the couple's children. Mr Tizard borrowed money using the house as security and Kingsnorth instructed a surveyor to visit the property on their behalf as part of the arrangements for the loan. The surveyor noticed that there was evidence of others living in the house but failed to make further enquiries about them and failed to report this to Kingsnorth. Mr Tizard eventually defaulted on his loan and Kingsnorth sought to take possession.

Decision

Mrs Tizard had acquired a constructive trust interest as a consequence of her financial contribution. Kingsnorth had imputed notice of that equitable interest as a consequence of the surveyor's inspection. Mrs Tizard's interest was therefore binding on them.

The effect of the 1925 legislation and the erosion of the doctrine of notice

The Law of Property Act 1925, you will remember, reduced the number of interests capable of existing as legal interests. As a consequence, the number of interests capable of existing as equitable interests necessarily increased and you might imagine that the doctrine of notice took on increased importance. However, one of the aims of the 1925 legislation was also to reduce the importance of the doctrine of notice. As a consequence, after 1925 equitable interests were treated in one of three ways, either as an interest registrable as a Land Charge, as an interest capable of being overreached or as an interest still subject to the doctrine of notice. We will deal with each in turn.

Interests capable of registration as Land Charges

The idea of a limited form of registration occurring in relation to unregistered title seems a little strange at first. It is important to recognise that this is *not* registration of title in the form that we encountered in Chapter 3. The system of Land Charges registration relates primarily to the registration of equitable interests affecting unregistered title. It is the interests themselves that are registered against the names of the owners of the land that is affected.

The Land Charges Act 1925 (since repealed and replaced with the Land Charges Act 1972) provides that where an interest is registered under the system it is deemed to constitute actual notice of that interest to third parties. This is obviously very important to both those who create the equitable interests as well as those third parties acquiring an estate in the land. It means that, provided the interest has been registered as a Land Charge, it will be binding on a purchaser. This applies whether or not the purchaser has made a search of the Land Charges Register and discovered the registration of the interest.

Equally, if an interest is capable of being registered as a Land Charge but it is not registered then it will be void against a purchaser for value of the legal estate. These are the consequences even if the buyer does know about the existence of the interest. In this case the issue of 'notice' becomes irrelevant.

On-the-spot question

? You are acting for a house builder who is interested in buying a piece of land that has an unregistered title. On reviewing the title deeds you notice that the land is subject to a restrictive covenant created in 1937 stating that nothing should be built on the land. The house that your client intends to build will potentially be in breach of that covenant. Your search of the Land Charges Register reveals that the restrictive covenant was not registered as a Land Charge. What are the consequences of the lack of registration for your client?

The system of Land Charges records equitable interests against landowners' names in 'classes' (see Figure 4.2). Some of the classes of Land Charge are more common than others and for the purposes of this chapter we will highlight only a few of the more significant ones.

Estate contract C(iv)
- A contract for the sale of land gives the buyer an equitable interest in that land which is capable of registration as a Land Charge.
- This class also relates to other contracts in relation to land including equitable leases.

Restrictive covenants (Dii)
- Promises not to do something in relation to land when properly created using the form of a deed are required to be protected by registration as a Land Charge.

'Home rights' (F)
- The rights of a spouse or civil partner to occupy the home are registrable as Land Charges.

Equitable easements (Diii)
- Easements are capable of existing as legal interests provided the appropriate formalities are met. Failure to comply with the formalities may result in an equitable easement being created, which is registrable as a Land Charge.

Figure 4.2 Examples of registrable Land Charges

There is one further interest that is worth noting here as an interest registrable as a Land Charge. It is dealt with separately because it is actually a *legal* interest and so is another anomaly in the law that students need to be aware of. It is called a 'puisne' mortgage and falls within Class C(i). A puisne mortgage is a second or subsequent legal mortgage. Where an unregistered title is subject to a mortgage it is the usual practice for the lender to retain the unregistered title deeds. However, if a borrower decides to take out further mortgages in relation to the land those subsequent lenders will not be able to take possession of the title deeds and must therefore protect their interest by registration of a Class C(i) Land Charge. The effects of registration/non-registration are exactly the same as for the equitable interests.

The need for a Land Charges search

Hopefully, an understanding of the consequences of non-registration of those equitable interests that are capable of being registered as Land Charges will make you appreciate how important it is for solicitors acting for buyers of unregistered title to make the appropriate searches of the Land Charges Register to check for those equitable (and occasionally legal) interests that might be protected. Remember that once registered a buyer is deemed to have actual notice of their existence, whether or not their solicitor makes a search of the register.

Usual practice in unregistered conveyancing is for the buyer's solicitor to either request a copy of previous Land Charges results from the seller's solicitor or to make their own search at the Land Charges Registry. Unlike the system of land registration where interests are registered against the title to the land itself, the system of Land Charges registration in unregistered land requires the Land Charges to be registered against the *names* of the landowners who were subject to the interest. It follows that when making a search of the Land Charges Register it is vitally important to search against an accurate version of the landowner's name (usually taken from the title deeds). Where the search result contains details of registrations protecting interests in relation to the land, the buyer's solicitor will check these against the title they have received and raise further enquiries of the seller's solicitors if more detail is required.

The principle of overreaching

In the same way that the system of Land Charges registration should not be confused with the much broader system of land registration, the principle of overreaching must not be confused with overriding interests (see Figure 4.3)!

Overriding interest	**Overreaching**
• Relates only to registered title. • Refers to the category of interests that do not require to be registered but are still binding on third parties.	• Relates to unregistered as well as registered land. • Allows buyers to buy land free from trust interests by paying the purchase price to a minimum of two trustees or a trust corporation.

Figure 4.3 A summary of the distinction between overriding interests and the principle of overreaching

Overreaching is not, in fact, an interest in land but rather a mechanism by which equitable interests under a trust can effectively be bypassed by a buyer. As a buyer of land you will be concerned to check the legal title of the person purporting to be able to sell to you and will have done this by a review of the title deeds. More difficult to check, however, are the rights of those who may have an equitable trust interest in relation to the property. From a very practical perspective you do not want to hand over a substantial amount of money to a seller who has effectively demonstrated their legal title and capacity to sell only to discover that there is another individual claiming equitable rights in the property who is challenging the sale.

The principle of overreaching means that where a buyer pays the purchase monies to two trustees, or a trust corporation, they will effectively leapfrog the beneficial interests of anyone with an interest under a trust and will take free of that interest, whether they knew about that interest or not. This is a relatively straightforward process. Assuming that there are two owners of the legal title there will automatically be two 'trustees'. As we shall see in Chapter 5, where there is more than one owner of a legal title there is automatically a trust. If there is only one legal title owner then in order to overreach any beneficial interests the owner will need to appoint someone to sit alongside them as a trustee and to receive the monies from the buyer. You might consider that this relatively easy way to bypass a beneficiary's interest in a property is unfair. However, the beneficiary does not lose all of their rights as a consequence of overreaching but instead those rights are transferred from the property itself to the purchase monies that have been paid. It should be noted that this mechanism for overreaching beneficiaries' interests can occur in relation to registered as well as unregistered land.

Interests still subject to the doctrine of notice

The Land Registration Act narrowed the categories of interest that are still capable of being subject to the doctrine of notice but there are still a number of interests that remain. In particular any restrictive covenants or equitable easements that were created before 1926 remain subject to the doctrine of notice as they predate the requirements for registration as Land Charges. Importantly constructive trust interests also remain subject to the doctrine of notice meaning that it is still very important to carry out thorough investigations of title and inspection of the land to check for non-owning adults in occupation. Bear in mind, however, that where a constructive trust exists it will still be possible to overreach that trust by payment of the purchase monies to two trustees.

SUMMARY

- Although the quantity of unregistered title in England and Wales is diminishing it is still important to be able to understand and apply the rules relating to the sale of unregistered land and the creation and protection of interests.
- Title to unregistered land is demonstrated by the production of deeds and documents creating a chain of ownership commencing with the 'root of title'.

- Legal interests in unregistered land are automatically binding on third parties.
- Since 1925 equitable interests in unregistered land fall into one of three categories: they can be protected by registration of a Land Charge, they can be overreached by payment of purchase monies to two trustees or a trust corporation or they can remain subject to the doctrine of notice.
- It is important when acting for a buyer of an unregistered title to undertake a thorough check of the title deeds, raise appropriate enquires of the seller and carry out a Land Charges search.

FURTHER READING

Abbey, R. and Richards, M., *A Practical Approach to Conveyancing*, 15th edn (Oxford University Press, 2014) – this book will give you an insight into how to demonstrate and review title to unregistered land from a practitioner's point of view.

Bray, J., *Unlocking Land Law*, 4th edn (Routledge, 2014) – this book offers a more detailed introduction to legal and equitable interests and the system of Land Charges registration.

Dixon, M., *Modern Land Law*, 9th edn (Routledge, 2014) – this book will give you a more detailed consideration of overreaching and how it relates to other aspects of this book, including co-ownership as well as a more detailed review of unregistered title.

Howell, J., 'The Doctrine of Notice: an historical perspective' [1997] *The Conveyancer and Property Lawyer* 341 – a useful review of the doctrine of notice and its application in relation to unregistered land.

Chapter 5
Co-ownership

LEARNING OBJECTIVES

After reading this chapter, you should be able to:

- appreciate that wherever there is more than one owner of a legal estate a trust is created;
- explain the different ways in which the legal and equitable titles to land can be held;
- distinguish between a joint tenancy and tenancy in common;
- recognise the methods of severing a joint tenancy;
- recognise the importance of the Trusts of Land and Appointment of Trustees Act 1996.

INTRODUCTION

The topic of co-ownership is one that many students can relate to and get to grips with relatively quickly. Key to an understanding of this topic is an appreciation of the importance of the trust and by now you will have an emerging knowledge of how equity operates alongside the common law rules, how the trust was developed by equity and the separation of legal and equitable titles where a trust exists.

This chapter will build on your foundational knowledge and explain the different ways in which the legal and equitable titles can be held and the implications of each. It will also introduce you to trusts of the family home and will look at the acquisition of equitable interests by those in occupation of property who do not hold legal title.

OWNERSHIP OF THE LEGAL ESTATE

In Chapter 2 we looked at the formalities required to be followed when title to land is transferred. You also now appreciate that following completion of the sale of property, title to the property will be registered (this now applies whether the original seller's title was registered or unregistered). The title that is registered reflects ownership of the *legal* estate in the land. So, if I were to buy the freehold of a new house and my solicitor, following completion, dealt with registration of my title my name would appear on the registers as the registered proprietor of the freehold estate in the land. I would be the legal title owner of the property.

The same principles apply where there is more than one person buying a property. If I had purchased the house together with my husband our solicitor could register both of our names as owners of the freehold legal estate and we would both appear on the registers of title.

The registration of my title to the land is, therefore, the public facing evidence of my ownership of the property (you will recall that the registers of title are open to public inspection). When I decide to sell the house the demonstration of my ability to sell will be the fact that I am registered as proprietor. I (and anyone else that is registered as a legal owner) will be required to sign the contract and transfer deed to give effect to the sale.

In theory, any number of people might own and have legal registered title to the same property. In practice the law allows only four names to be registered as legal owners of the property (this is the effect of s.34 (2) Law of Property Act 1925). This does not mean that it is not possible to have more than four legal owners, but simply that the first four names on the document that transfers title will be registered.

This consideration of ownership and transfer of the legal estate is quite straightforward. Things become a little more complicated, however, when you imagine a scenario where the co-owners of the property have different interests in relation to that property. So, what would happen if the buyers of a property were business partners rather than husband and wife? They may well both be registered as proprietors of the property but are likely to want their interests in the property separately recorded – perhaps because they contributed differing amounts to the purchase price. On a sale of that property they may want to be sure that the proceeds of sale would be split between them according to the proportions of the purchase price that they contributed. Similarly, a previously divorced couple with children from their previous marriages who purchase property together may want to ensure that their children are provided for in the event of their death. They may want to leave their share of the property through their will, for example.

From a buyer's perspective, the personal arrangements of the co-owners should not really be of any concern. If I were buying the property from the business partners I would want to ensure that both entered into the contract for the sale of the property and that vacant possession of the property was given on completion, but I would not be interested in what happened to the proceeds of sale once I had paid them over. My interest is primarily in the legal title to the property and the capacity of those registered proprietors to sell.

EQUITABLE OWNERSHIP

It is therefore in equity that the respective shares of the owners of property are recognised. Wherever there is more than one legal owner of property a trust will automatically be created and there will be a separation of the outward, public facing legal title and, behind the trust, an equitable title (sometimes referred to as the beneficial title). It is the equitable title that is often described as giving the true reflection of the ownership rights of those with an interest in the property.

In the example of the business partners, then, the legal title demonstrates their co-ownership of the property and alerts a buyer to the need to enter into a contract with both of them. The equitable title also confirms their co-ownership but allows them to distinguish their separate shares of the property, based, for example, on their respective contributions towards the original purchase price.

On-the-spot question

 What might the nature of the legal and equitable titles be in relation to the previously divorced couple?

TYPES OF CO-OWNERSHIP

There are two types of co-ownership that are capable of existing: the joint tenancy and the tenancy in common. As a student of land law you will need to be familiar with both and we will consider each in turn.

Joint tenancy

The first thing to note is that a joint tenancy has nothing to do with a tenancy in the context of the leasehold estate in land. The concept of a joint tenancy is quite different and relates to the way in which property is co-owned. A joint tenancy treats co-owners as though they were one single entity rather than separate owners with distinct rights and interests. If I were to own my house jointly with my husband as joint tenants then the law would view us as one unit. I could not, for example, claim that we owned the property 50/50 as this would suggest the existence of half shares in the property. Instead we are each entitled to the whole of the property.

The legal title to property can only be held by co-owners as joint tenants. This is the effect of s.34(2) of the Law of Property Act 1925. It means that notwithstanding that there might be up to four names registered as legal title owners they will all be treated as though they are one unit. This has the advantage of keeping the legal title relatively straightforward. One of the consequences of this is that if one of those legal co-owners were to die the legal title would simply be absorbed by the remaining co-owners. This is known as the principle of survivorship.

Key definition: Survivorship

When a joint tenant dies they have no separate interest to dispose of. Instead, the surviving joint tenant(s) simply continue(s) to own the property and the deceased drops out of the picture.

In order to create a joint tenancy there is a requirement that the 'four unities' are present. The four unities are unity of possession, interest, title and time. Unity of possession requires each joint tenant to be entitled to possession of the whole of the property. In a domestic situation this unity will almost certainly always be present. It is unlikely that one co-owner would, or indeed could, exclude the other from part of the house. Unity of interest means that each of the co-owners must have the same rights in respect of the property. So, where a landlord owns the freehold of a property and grants a lease to another individual there is no unity of interest (because they own different estates in land) and therefore there is no joint tenancy and, indeed, no co-ownership. Unity of title means that each joint tenant must have acquired their interest in the property through the same means. Ordinarily this would be satisfied where co-purchasers sign the same transfer deed. Finally, unity of time means that the interests must have been created contemporaneously. So, assuming co-purchasers signed the same transfer deed (and created a unity of interest) and the transfer deed was dated to give effect to completion of a purchase then there will be unity of time.

Where one or more of the four unities is not present, then a joint tenancy has not been created. In that case the second of the two types of co-ownership will exist, the tenancy in common, which is discussed below.

On-the-spot question

? After graduating from university, three friends pool their resources and buy the freehold of a Victorian townhouse together. They each have separate bedrooms within the house but share the kitchen, bathroom and living areas. Do they have unity of possession?

Tenancy in common

A tenancy in common is distinct from a joint tenancy in that it enables co-owners to hold distinct shares in the property. Only one of the four unities is required to be present, unity of possession. It remains the case that while tenants in common may have separate interests in the property it is not possible to physically divide the property and exclude co-owners from it.

A tenancy in common cannot be created in respect of the legal title. In equity, both the joint tenancy and tenancy in common are capable of existing. Where there is a tenancy in common the co-owners will hold distinct shares in the property that are capable of being disposed of in a number of ways. It is possible to leave the shares in the property in a will, for example, so that when one of the co-owners dies they can provide for beneficiaries. The business owners who contributed different amounts to the purchase price of a property will be able to take out their respective shares on any subsequent sale.

DETERMINING OWNERSHIP OF THE EQUITABLE TITLE

If the legal title to the property is the outward facing demonstration of ownership, then how is equitable ownership of the property established? We have noted that wherever co-owners purchase property a trust is automatically created, but how do we know whether the equitable title is held as a joint tenancy or a tenancy in common?

Most co-owners will make a declaration of their intentions regarding the equitable title when they purchase. By doing this they will have expressly created the trust and stated the nature of the equitable title. The standard documentation used by the Land Registry invites purchasers to declare whether they hold as joint tenants or tenants in common and, if the latter, whether in equal shares or otherwise. If more complex arrangements need to be recorded or the arrangements are agreed after the purchase of the property has been completed then the co-owners can enter into a declaration of trust, a legal document that records the financial arrangements of the parties and the shares in the property that have been created as a consequence of the trust.

In the more unusual situations where co-owners have failed to identify the means by which they will own the equitable title it may be left to the courts to determine whether there is a joint tenancy or tenancy in common. In this case the equitable ownership will be implied. Generally, the accepted rule has been that 'equity follows the law'. This means that as the legal title is held by co-owners as joint tenants so the equitable title must be held in the same way. However, there are numerous exceptions to this rule. In our example of the business partners there will likely be a presumption of a tenancy in common unless the parties have expressly agreed otherwise because of the nature of their relationship. In relation to a purchase of a family home *Stack v Dowden* reinforced the traditional rule but accepted that the presumption could be rebutted based on the presumed intention of the parties based on their course of dealings.

KEY CASE ANALYSIS: *Stack v Dowden* [2007] 2 AC 432

Background

Mr Stack and Ms Dowden lived together with four children. At first they lived in a house belonging to Ms Dowden but subsequently moved to a house that they purchased together and which they co-owned. No declaration had been made as to beneficial ownership. Ms Dowden had contributed the larger share of the purchase price, using the proceeds of sale from her previous property. The relationship broke down and the House of Lords had to decide whether Mr Stack was entitled to an equal half share or whether Ms Dowden should be awarded a greater share as a consequence of her larger contribution to the purchase price.

Decision

The House of Lords held that Ms Dowden should be awarded a greater share of the interest as she had rebutted the presumption that there should be joint beneficial ownership. The circumstances of the case implied an intention to hold in different shares.

Although a buyer of property is ordinarily only concerned with the names of the legal title owners to property it is sometimes necessary for solicitors acting for a buyer to check the nature of the equitable ownership. An example is where one of the registered proprietors is deceased and a buyer is purchasing from the survivor. We have established that the legal title must always be held as a joint tenancy and so on the death of one of the co-owners the rule of survivorship will apply and the deceased simply disappears from the picture. However, if in equity the co-owners had held as tenants in common it is possible that the deceased's share of the property has been left to other beneficiaries. A solicitor acting for the buyer will want to ensure that their client is able to purchase the property without the risk of third parties raising a claim in respect of the property as a consequence of being left a share in the property through a will.

In registered title the presence of a tenancy in common is identified by a restriction on the proprietorship register of the title.

Key definition: Restriction

An entry made in the title registers that prevents or restricts the registration of a disposal of the registered estate.

The restriction reads: 'No disposition by a sole proprietor of the registered estate (except a trust corporation) under which capital money arises is to be registered unless authorised by an order of the court.' While the restriction does not refer specifically to a tenancy in common (and in fact the Land Registry uses this restriction for a number of purposes), it is an indication that the equitable title may need closer inspection. Generally speaking in the absence of a restriction a solicitor will assume that a joint tenancy existed and will ask for evidence of death, (through a death certificate) and will proceed on the basis that survivorship applies.

In unregistered title the title deeds will need to be reviewed to look for declarations as to equitable ownership.

The solution to the problem of equitable interests and how to bypass them comes in a principle that we introduced in Chapter 4, the principle of overreaching.

Key definition: Overreaching

Where a buyer pays the purchase monies to two trustees, or a trust corporation, they will take free from the beneficial interests of anyone with an interest under a trust.

On-the-spot question

? A solicitor acting for a buyer of a property discovers that one of two registered legal co-owners is deceased. On checking the registered title the solicitor notes that a restriction has been registered protecting an equitable tenancy in common. What steps must they now take?

Remember that where overreaching occurs the interests of any beneficial owners (those who have inherited property as a consequence of a will for example) will not be extinguished but will transfer from the property itself into the proceeds of sale. The result of the principle of overreaching means that the buyer can effectively ignore the beneficial entitlement and will take free of any equitable interests.

SEVERANCE OF A JOINT TENANCY

While the legal title to property must always be held by co-owners as joint tenants it is possible to convert a joint tenancy of the equitable title into a tenancy in common through the principle of severance. There are a number of reasons why co-owners might want to convert a joint tenancy into a tenancy in common but often this will result from a breakdown of a relationship that prompts co-owners to want to determine their precise shares in the property.

There are a number of accepted ways of severing a joint tenancy and each will be covered in turn.

Severance by written notice

s.36(2) of the Law of Property Act 1925 allows any beneficial joint tenant wanting to sever the joint tenancy in equity to give written notice of their intention to the other joint tenants. There is no prescribed form for the notice and no requirement that the other joint tenants must agree to the severance. There must, however, be evidence of a clear intention to sever. There are a number of cases where the courts have been required to consider documents purporting to give effect to severance and to decide whether sufficient evidence of intention has been present.

KEY CASE ANALYSIS: *Harris v Goddard* [1983] 1 WLR 1203

Background

A married couple's relationship broke down and the wife began divorce proceedings. As part of the proceedings an application was made for a property adjustment order (an order by the court as to shares in the property) in relation to the matrimonial home that the couple held as beneficial joint tenants. The wording of the application was broad and did not specifically refer to severance of the joint tenancy. While the divorce proceedings were continuing the husband died. The courts had to determine whether prior to the husband's death the joint tenancy had been severed by the application.

Decision

The Court of Appeal held that there had not been severance because there was no evidence of an immediate intention to sever the joint tenancy. The application for the property adjustment order was a request to the court to make the order and not sufficient to immediately sever the joint tenancy.

In other cases the courts have had to consider whether the written notice was effectively served on the other joint tenants. The service of notices is covered by s.196 of the Law of Property Act 1925, which requires notices to be in writing and states that notices shall be sufficiently served if left at the last known place of abode or business or if sent by registered post (provided the notice is not returned as undelivered). The leading cases that deal with service of notices intending to sever a joint tenancy involve circumstances where there is some dispute as to whether the notice was received or not.

KEY CASE ANALYSIS: *Re 88 Berkley Road* [1971] Ch 648

Background

Two elderly ladies were joint tenants of their shared home. One of the ladies decided to marry and the other instructed solicitors to sever the joint tenancy, who then sent a notice of severance by recorded delivery. In fact it was the lady who had instructed her solicitors to sever who was at home when the letter arrived. She signed for it and shortly afterwards died. The surviving lady claimed that she had never seen the letter and that therefore there could be no severance.

Decision

The Court held that the notice having been sent by recorded delivery, there was sufficient service for the purposes of s.36(2) and s.196(4) of the Law of Property Act 1925 and that severance had therefore occurred notwithstanding that the intended recipient had not herself signed for and received the letter.

A useful comparison is the subsequent case of *Kinch v Bullard*.

KEY CASE ANALYSIS: *Kinch v Bullard* [1999] 1 WLR 423

Background

A married couple's relationship broke down and the wife instructed solicitors to serve a notice of severance that was served by ordinary post. The husband was taken into hospital before he read the letter and the wife found the letter at home and destroyed it. The husband died a short time later and the wife herself subsequently died some months afterwards. The court had to decide whether the letter had been sufficient to sever the joint tenancy.

Decision

The Court held that the notice was sufficient to sever the joint tenancy. Despite the letter having been sent by ordinary post rather than recorded delivery there was evidence that it had been received and therefore satisfied the requirement of s.196(3) that the letter had been left at the last known place of abode. It did not matter, in those circumstances, that the husband had never read the letter.

Whether or not a notice is deemed to be sufficient to sever will determine what happens to the property in the event of the death of one or more of the co-owners. In the *Kinch v Bullard* case, for example, the effect of the notice having been effectively served meant that the joint tenancy had been severed prior to the husband's death. This meant that he had a distinct share in the property capable of being left through his will. If the notice had not been effectively served then the rule of survivorship would have applied and his wife would have automatically become the sole owner of the property. The implications, then, are potentially huge for the parties involved and one reason why best advice is to very clearly state an immediate intention to sever in a written notice and to ensure that this is served personally or by recorded delivery.

Severance by mutual agreement

We have seen that written notice to sever can be made unilaterally – in other words without the agreement of the other joint tenants. It is, however, possible to sever a joint tenancy by mutual agreement of the parties. Importantly, where severance takes place by mutual agreement there is no need for writing.

An example of severance by mutual agreement can be found in the case of *Burgess v Rawnsley*.

KEY CASE ANALYSIS: *Burgess v Rawnsley* [1975] 1 Ch 429

Background

A couple purchased a property jointly but following the breakdown of the relationship one agreed orally to buy the other's share in the property. The agreement was never recorded in writing and in fact there was some negotiation about the price that would be paid. Before the negotiation was concluded the intended buyer of the share died. The intended seller claimed to have decided not to proceed on the basis of the oral agreement.

Decision

The Court held that the mutual agreement between the parties was sufficient to sever the joint tenancy even though the agreement had been oral and informally reached and the price had not been settled.

It is important to note that in *Burgess v Rawnsley* the court was able to find evidence of an agreement, even though the price payable was in dispute. Where there are ongoing negotiations about whether or not to sever this will almost inevitably mean that there will be no severance.

Severance by a course of dealing

This method of severance occurs when all of the joint tenants act in such a way as to treat the joint tenancy as at an end. As a consequence, courts have found there to be a 'common intention' to sever. There is some overlap here with severance by mutual agreement and, indeed, in the case of *Burgess v Rawnsley* referred to above Lord Denning found that even had there not been an agreement to sell the shares the mere fact of their negotiations would have been enough to sever. This view, however, was not widely supported and it remains the case that it would be very difficult to prove severance of a joint tenancy on the basis of continuing negotiations that have not been concluded.

Severance by acting on one's own share

The essence of this method is quite straightforward. It essentially means that if a joint tenant acts in a way that is inconsistent with the existence of a joint tenancy then this may be sufficient to sever the joint tenancy.

The most obvious way of acting on one's own share would be to sell your interest in the land to a third party. Remember that there cannot be severance of the legal title and so this would mean disposing of an equitable interest in the property. Ignoring the practical difficulties of doing this (it is difficult to imagine that in a domestic situation one of the co-owners might be able to find someone willing to take a transfer of an equitable share in the family home), the act of disposing of an interest would inevitably result in the severance of the joint tenancy, in order to create the share that is then transferred. There would be a similar result if one co-owning joint tenant sold their share to another joint tenant of the same property or indeed mortgaged their interest.

TRUSTS OF LAND AND APPOINTMENT OF TRUSTEES ACT 1996

Where there is co-ownership there is always a trust. This means that the legal title owners effectively hold the property on trust for the beneficiaries, who hold the equitable title. Throughout this chapter we have tended to focus on a situation where the legal and beneficial title holders are, in fact, the same people but of course this doesn't necessarily need to be the case. It is perfectly possible for the legal title holders to hold the property on trust for others, for example where a deceased's estate is held by trustees for the benefit of the deceased's spouse and children.

Whether the legal and equitable titles are held by the same or different people it remains the case that the trustees of the land have both rights and responsibilities in relation to that land. Those rights and responsibilities are now governed by the Trusts of Land and Appointment of Trustees Act 1996 (TOLATA) which introduced the concept of the 'trust of land'.

The development of the trust of land and the detailed provisions of TOLATA are outside the scope of this book but it is important to recognise that the trustees may deal with the land as absolute owners but have a duty to consult the beneficiaries where it is practicable to do so and to give effect to the wishes of the beneficiaries where they are 'consistent with the general interest of the trust' (s.11(1) TOLATA 1996).

Importantly, the courts also have a jurisdiction to intervene where there are disputes about the trust of land. Under s.14 of TOLATA, the trustees or beneficiaries may make an application to court for an order relating to the exercise by the trustees of any of their functions or to declare the nature and extent of a person's interest in the property. The courts will take a number of factors into account before making an order, particularly if the order sought is one of sale of the property.

TRUSTS OF THE FAMILY HOME

Finally, in this chapter we return to the concept of trusts of the family home. While this is not directly related to the purchase of property by co-owners it does have direct links to this chapter in that often it may result in co-ownership of the equitable title.

We have looked at examples where co-purchasers acquire the legal title and as a result a trust is automatically created (as was the case in *Stack v Dowden*). It would also be possible for an individual to acquire a legal title in their own name but to hold the property on trust for themselves and others. This could be created expressly using the declaration of trust document that we referred to earlier in the chapter.

Often, however, these types of trust and co-ownership of the equitable title arise impliedly out of the actions of the parties involved. We saw in Chapter 4 the means by which an individual can acquire an equitable interest in property by virtue of their contributing to the purchase price or mortgage repayments, notwithstanding that they may not be a legal owner of the property. This was the case in *Kingsnorth Finance Co Ltd v Tizard*. This was an example of a constructive trust interest where the court was able to infer a common intention based on the circumstances of the case. The application of the law relating to constructive trusts (and resulting trusts where a beneficial interest is acquired by a person who has contributed directly to the purchase of a property but is not registered as proprietor) is outside the scope of this book but you can read about this further in *Beginning Equity and Trusts.*

SUMMARY

- Wherever there are co-owners of property there is a trust and a separation of the legal and equitable titles.
- The legal title can only ever be held by co-owners as joint tenants but the equitable title can be held as joint tenants or tenants in common.
- The nature of the equitable ownership may be expressly declared or may be implied based on the presumed intention of the parties.
- A joint tenancy in equity may be severed in certain circumstances, turning it into a tenancy in common.
- The rights and responsibilities of the legal title owners as trustees are governed by the Trusts of Land and Appointment of Trustees Act 1996.

FURTHER READING

Gravells, N. P., 'Severance of a Joint Tenancy: a land law "Whodunnit?"' (2012) *Cambridge Law Journal*, 71 – a review of a recent case, *Quigley v Masterson [2011] EWHC 2529 (Ch)*, that raised a typical dispute around severance.

Law Society and Land Registry Practice Note: Joint Ownership: www.landregistry.gov.uk/professional/about-us/policy-statements/law-society-joint-ownership-practice-note – a useful summary of the position where there is no express declaration of trust and practice advice to solicitors acting for co-purchasers.

Pawlowski, M., 'Imputed intention and joint ownership – a return to common sense: *Jones v Kernott*' [2012] *The Conveyancer and Property Lawyer* 2 – discussion of the nature and consideration of intention when determining beneficial shares in property.

Ramjohn, M., *Beginning Equity and Trusts*, 1st edn (Routledge 2013) – contains a more detailed introduction to resulting and constructive trusts.

Warner-Reed, E., *Optimize Land Law*, 1st edn (Routledge, 2014) – this book has a useful summary of the informal creation of a trust of land.

Chapter 6
Leaseholds

LEARNING OBJECTIVES

After reading this chapter, you should be able to:

- appreciate the importance of the leasehold estate in land;
- explain the essential requirements for the leasehold to exist;
- identify the appropriate formalities for the creation of a lease;
- compare and contrast leases and licences.

INTRODUCTION

Many of us at some point in our lives will come across the leasehold interest in land. During your years at university you may well sign tenancy agreements with landlords allowing you to rent a home that you share with friends while you are studying. You might at some point buy a house that is a leasehold, perhaps with a very long lease in place where any rent that is payable is nominal. You may at some point even purchase property for investment purposes and yourself become a landlord of a rented property.

As with many other aspects of land law you may well already have preconceived ideas about what the study of leaseholds is all about. This chapter will help you to develop the foundational knowledge of the leasehold estate, how leases are created and the differences between leases and licences on which to build with your studies of land law.

DEFINITIONS

In essence, a lease is a form of contract. In a land law context, under the terms of that contract, an owner of land grants rights of occupation to a third party for a defined period of time. These rights can be granted for short or very long periods. Often the terminology used to describe the arrangement differs depending on the nature of the agreement. So, a short term lease of property, say for six months, is often called a tenancy whereas a longer arrangement, perhaps a grant of rights for 99 years, is called a lease. A tenancy, then, is a form of lease and the terms are often used interchangeably.

In legal terms the definition of a lease is a little more detailed. This is because a lease is not only a contract but is also capable of existing as one of the two legal estates in land. You will remember that the Law of Property Act 1925 recognises two legal estates, the fee simple absolute in possession, (the freehold) and the term of years absolute (the leasehold). The reference to 'term of years' is important because one of the hallmarks of the leasehold estate is that it is time limited. Once the leasehold term has expired, the estate will cease to exist and any title in the property that was held by the leasehold owner will revert to the owner of the freehold estate from which the leasehold was created. Interestingly, although the terminology used by the Law of Property Act 1925 refers to a term of *years*, the definition of this term in s.205(1)(xxvii) of the Act makes it clear that the term is capable of being less than a year or a fraction of a year so in theory a lease of property for a week only is technically possible.

On-the-spot question

 Do you think that an arrangement whereby a freehold estate owner agrees to allow a student friend the right to occupy the house 'for as long as you are a student' is capable of existing as a lease?

It is important to be familiar with some of the terminology used in relation to leaseholds. Figure 6.1 aims to set out some of the more common terms.

Leasehold estates are also capable of being sold. Imagine that you had acquired a 999 year lease of a flat in London and had paid a considerable premium as part of the transaction. Arguably, a lease of that length is virtually as good as ownership of a freehold estate and so it is important that the interest you have acquired is marketable and that you are able to dispose of it freely. In the example if you wanted to move away from the flat you may not want to sub-let the property (which would result in you retaining an interest and potentially a liability in relation to the flat), but rather you may want to dispose of the interest altogether. This is called an 'assignment' of the lease and in that scenario the tenant becomes an 'assignor' and the purchaser of the leasehold estate is the 'assignee'. In commercial conveyancing landlords often want to retain control over how and to whom a tenant is entitled to assign their lease but in residential transactions tenants should usually be able to do this freely (subject, of course, to any restrictions imposed by a mortgage).

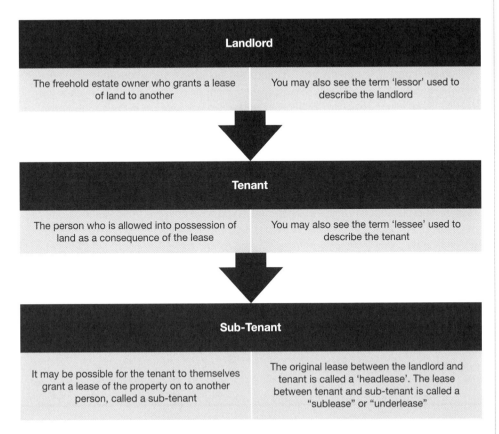

Figure 6.1 An explanation of some key terms relating to leaseholds

Finally, it is also important to recognise that the lease, as an estate in land, is a proprietary interest. On the sale of the freehold estate out of which the lease has been granted, the buyer of the freehold will take subject to the lease interest. It is important to make the distinction between a lease and a licence arrangement. The latter creates only a personal right that does not attach to the land itself and is therefore vulnerable to termination and will not, on the face of it, bind a buyer of the freehold estate.

WHY CREATE A LEASE?

Having indicated that ownership of a 999 year lease is arguably almost as good as ownership of the freehold you might be asking yourself why an owner of a freehold would create a lease rather than just selling the freehold estate itself. There are a number of reasons why landlords grant leases, some of which are practical and commercial and some of which are legal. From a landlord's perspective, creating a lease might be an investment opportunity. In shorter commercial leases, for example, landlords receive a rent from the leased properties while retaining a valuable interest in the freehold. This is known as a reversionary interest, in other words an interest in land that reverts back to the landlord once the leasehold estate ceases to exist (which might be on the expiry of the lease term or earlier depending on the circumstances). In this context a tenant might also prefer to take a lease interest rather than purchase the freehold because it offers a shorter term commitment which potentially carries less risk.

From a legal perspective leases are often granted to ensure that positive obligations entered into in respect of the property are capable of binding future purchasers of the property. This concept will become clearer once you have covered the chapter on covenants but an example here will hopefully help you to appreciate why leaseholds are so important in this regard. Imagine that you are the owner and developer of a building that is subdivided into flats. In order to ensure that the building is properly maintained and the flats are kept in a good condition you want to impose obligations onto the buyers of the flat to keep the interior of the flats in good repair and to contribute towards the costs of maintenance of those parts of the building that are shared (the stairwells, gardens, external decoration of the building and so on). All of the obligations are positive in nature (in order to comply, the buyers have to actually *do* something). They will be drafted into the legal documentation as covenants.

Key definition: Covenant

A promise made in the form of a deed. Covenants can be restrictive (i.e. *not* to do something) or positive (i.e. a positive obligation *to* do something).

As you will see in Chapter 9, the creation of a positive covenant is binding on the original parties to it. So, on the sale of a freehold estate where a positive covenant has been imposed (perhaps an obligation to maintain a boundary structure) the buyer of the freehold who agreed to the covenant is bound by it and can be held liable to the seller if there is a breach of it. The difficulty in freehold conveyancing arises when the buyer who gave the covenant sells on. There is no means in law by which the burden of that freehold covenant can automatically pass on to the successor in title, which can create problems in relation to enforceability.

In leasehold conveyancing, however, it has long been the case that positive covenants are enforceable against successors in title. For this reason, where there are likely to be ongoing positive obligations in relation to a property it makes sense for the freeholder owner to grant a long leasehold interest rather than to sell the freehold itself.

THE ESSENTIAL REQUIREMENTS FOR A LEASE

Key definition: Lease

'A contract for the exclusive possession and profit of land for some determinate period.'

per Lord Templeman in *Prudential Assurance v London Residuary Body* [1992] 2 AC 386

We have looked in general terms at the nature of the lease and the leasehold estate in land. Now we must consider how a lease is distinguished from other types of interest in relation to land and the essential requirements that must be present for a lease to exist.

The quote from Lord Templeman above emphasises the contractual nature of a lease but also sets out two other key requirements that must be considered when determining whether there is a lease in existence. Those are exclusive possession and a determinate period. We will look at these in turn and will also briefly consider the payment of rent as a factor in determining whether a lease is present.

Determinate period

We have already looked at the nature of the leasehold estate as a term of years absolute. Implicit in the terminology is the notion that a lease has to have a specified start and end date. This requirement is perhaps best illustrated by reference to examples from case law.

KEY CASE ANALYSIS: *Lace v Chantler* [1944] KB 368

Background

A house was subject to a tenancy agreement that was to last 'for the duration of the war'.

Decision

Lord Greene (MR) said: 'A term created by a leasehold tenancy agreement must be expressed either with certainty and specifically or by reference to something which can, at the time when the lease takes effect, be looked to as a certain ascertainment of what the term is meant to be.' In this case the term was uncertain and it was impossible to say how long the tenancy would last. The lease was, therefore, void. (Note, though that subsequent special legislation converted leases for the duration of the war into leases granted for 10 years in order to avoid this problem.)

In the later case of *Prudential Assurance v London Residuary Body* the lease was granted until such time as the land that was the subject of the lease was required by the County Council for the purpose of road widening works. In fact the road widening works never took place and the land was sold, the new owner seeking to terminate the lease. The tenants argued that the lease could not be brought to an end until such time as the land was required for road widening. The House of Lords held that the lease was void for lack of certain duration. However, the lease did not fail altogether. By virtue of the tenant's possession of the land and payment of a yearly rent, the Court found that the tenant was holding under a yearly tenancy a valid lease, but one that was able to be terminated on six months' notice. The reasons why the lease was rescued in this way will be discussed shortly.

There are a number of other occasions where statute has intervened to save what would otherwise be leases that are void for lack of certain duration. Examples are leases that are granted for the life of the tenant or leases that are granted until the tenant should marry (or enter into a civil partnership). The Law of Property Act 1925 (as amended) provides that such leases shall be deemed to have been granted for a term of 90 years, but subject to earlier termination on the death, marriage or civil partnership of the tenant. The result is that they are deemed to have a fixed maximum duration (but can be brought to an end earlier).

Exclusive possession

Arguably the concept of exclusive possession lies at the heart of the landlord and tenant relationship and is something that must always be considered when assessing whether a valid lease has been created.

The starting point for a discussion of the requirements of exclusive possession is almost always the case of *Street v Mountford*.

KEY CASE ANALYSIS: *Street v Mountford* **[1985] AC 809**

Background

Mr Street granted Mrs Mountford the right to occupy two rooms for £37 per week subject to termination on 14 days' written notice. The agreement that was signed was described as a licence. Mrs Mountford and her husband moved into the rooms and enjoyed exclusive occupation of them. The House of Lords had to decide whether the agreement between the parties was a licence or whether in reality they had entered into a lease arrangement.

Decision

Where residential accommodation had been granted at a rent with exclusive possession the nature of the true arrangement between the parties was that of a lease, notwithstanding that the agreement was actually described as a licence.

The test of exclusive possession is therefore one of substance and not form. The principle confirmed in *Street v Mountford* indicates that we should ignore the labels that are attached to agreements of this type and examine the true nature of the relationship between the parties. In doing this, Lord Templeman drew a simple distinction between a tenant and a lodger, saying:

> the occupier is a lodger if the landlord provides attendance or services which require the landlord or his servants to exercise unrestricted access to and use of the premises. A lodger is entitled to live in the premises but cannot call the place his own.

It follows, therefore, that if the tenant is entitled to enjoy full possession of the property with the landlord only reserving rights of entry to examine the repair or carry out maintenance then that tenant will enjoy exclusive possession and will have a lease. In *Street v Mountford*, Mr Street had not provided any services and had only reserved limited rights of inspection and maintenance. Mrs Mountford, therefore, had to be a tenant.

The concept of exclusive possession was further developed in two cases that have come to be known as 'the 1988 cases'. The House of Lords gave judgment in both cases on the same day and the facts and decisions of the two cases are very useful in any analysis of whether an arrangement is a licence or a lease.

KEY CASE ANALYSIS: *Antoniades v Villiers* [1990] 1 AC 417

Background

A young couple signed agreements for the occupation of a small one-bedroom flat on the same day. Each of them signed a separate agreement stating that they were personal licences only and offered no grant of exclusive possession. The owner of the property stated that they had the right to use the rooms in common with the couple and the right to allow others to do so also.

Decision

The House of Lords found that the two agreements should not be read as separate and independent licences. The couple had applied jointly to occupy the property and should be treated as such. The provision that they allow the owner to share occupation of the property was a pretence. The property was not suitable for occupation for any more than one couple.

The House of Lords considered the practical realities of the situation in *Antoniades v Villiers*. It was the couple's intention to share occupation of the flat as would a married couple. Given the choice of having the bedroom furnished with either two single beds or a double bed they chose a double bed. One would not have signed the agreement for occupation without the other and the agreements were identical and signed on the same day. Lord Oliver of Aylmerton described the 'total air of unreality' about the separate nature of the documents signed given the circumstances of the case. As a consequence the House of Lords treated the couple as though they were joint tenants with all four unities present and with exclusive possession. They were therefore tenants.

KEY CASE ANALYSIS: *AG Securities v Vaughan and others* [1988] 1 AC 417

Background

Four individual occupants were each granted a licence agreement to share a flat with others, offering no exclusive possession of the property. The property in question was a four bedroom property with associated rooms. The occupants had signed separate agreements on different dates, for different terms and with varying rents. The occupants at the time had all replaced earlier occupants of the property who had left.

Decision

The House of Lords found that a lease had not been created. These were four separate licences granted to separate individuals at different times and on different terms. There was no single sum of money paid for the occupation and no one 'single indivisible' term.

The facts of *AG Securities v Vaughan* are obviously quite different to those in *Antoniades v Villiers* and the decisions reflect a common sense approach to the different circumstances. The House of Lords found that in *AG Securities v Vaughan* the four unities could not be said to be present and that therefore you could not consider the occupants of the property to constitute a single collective tenancy in the way that they had been able to do with the couple in *Antoniades v Villiers*.

On-the-spot question

 Do you think that the decision in *Antoniades v Villiers* would have been different if the couple had been paying different amounts under the agreements that they signed and had entered into the agreements on different dates?

Before leaving the discussion on exclusive possession it is worth briefly mentioning other specific circumstances that a court might take into account when deciding whether or not an arrangement is that of a lodger or tenant. The first is where a person is allowed into occupation of property as a result of an act of generosity or friendship. In *Rhodes v Dalby* [1971] 1 WLR 1325 a friend was allowed into occupation of a bungalow while the owner was abroad on the basis of a 'gentleman's agreement'. Rent was paid during his occupation but the Court of Appeal found that the nature of the agreement was such that there had been no intention to create legal relations and therefore there could be no lease. Similarly, allowing an employee into occupation of a residence associated with their employment is unlikely to be treated as a lease. In *Crane v Morris* [1965] 1 WLR 1104 a farm worker was allowed to occupy a cottage on the farm during his employment. The Court of Appeal found that this was a licence that came to an end when the employee finished his service.

Finally, the courts have had to consider whether the retention of a freehold owner of the keys to a property points towards the creation of a licence rather than a lease. In *Aslan v*

Murphy [1990] 1 WLR 766 a basement flat, suitable only for occupation by one person, was occupied under an agreement described as a licence that allowed the owner to retain keys and required the occupant to vacate the room for 90 minutes every day. These provisions were held by the Court of Appeal to be sham provisions as during the occupation virtually no services had been provided by the owner. The situation would have been different if there had been a genuine requirement for the retention of the keys for the provision of daily services.

Rent

In *Street v Mountford* Lord Templeman noted that for a valid lease to exist there had to be exclusive possession for a defined term and in consideration of a premium or periodic payments. Most short term leases will be granted subject to the payment of a periodic rent, whether that is weekly, monthly or even annually. Where much longer leases are granted the rent may be nominal and instead the tenant may have paid a sum of money up-front in consideration of the grant of the lease. This is known as a premium and is reflective of the fact that long leases are marketable interests in land.

The definition of a 'term of years' contained in s.205(1)(xxvii) of the Law of Property Act 1925, however, makes no reference to rent being a requirement and the case of *Ashburn Anstalt v Arnold* [1989] Ch. 1 held that where a lease was granted for a certain term with exclusive possession the absence of rent would not be an issue. It would appear, therefore, that rent is not a significant factor in determining whether a lease has been created.

THE FORMALITIES FOR THE CREATION OF A LEASE

We began this chapter by stating that a lease was a form of contract. The nature of the contract formed is that of a 'conveyance' and you will recall that in Chapter 2 we looked at 'conveyancing' as being the means by which ownership in land is transferred. In the case of a lease, the transfer is that of a leasehold estate out of a freehold estate, leaving the tenant the owner of the lease and the landlord the owner of the freehold reversion. The formalities required to give effect to this conveyance or transfer require the use of a deed, under s.52 of the Law of Property Act 1925. We looked at the requirements for a valid deed in Chapter 2.

There is, however, an exception to the rule that leases must be created in the form of a deed. As a consequence of s.54(2) of the Law of Property Act 1925 leases granted for a term of three years or less are not required to be made by deed, or indeed even in writing provided they are granted for the best rent reasonable obtainable.

There is one further formality that must be remembered in relation to the creation of leaseholds. Any lease granted for a term of more than seven years must be registered in order to be treated as a legal lease. This is the effect of s.4(1)(c) and s.27(1) and (2)(b) of the Land Registration Act 2002.

Figure 6.2 sets out the basic requirements.

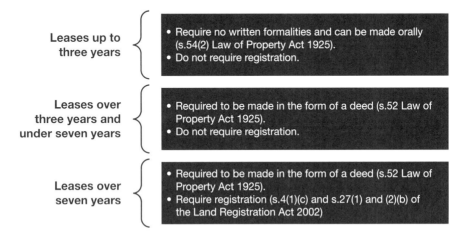

Figure 6.2 The basic requirements for registration of leases

On-the-spot question

You act for a client who has been granted a lease out of a registered freehold estate for a fixed term of five years. The lease has been granted using the appropriate formalities of a deed. Are you required to register the leasehold estate and, if not, how will it be protected as an interest in land?

Equitable leases

As we have seen in earlier chapters equity will often intervene to mitigate the harshness of the common law rules. The law in relation to leaseholds is no different. On the face of it, failure to comply with the formalities for the creation of a lease should result in the lease being treated as void. However, in certain circumstances an equitable lease may be created. This will occur where, for example, the document purporting to give effect to the creation of a leasehold estate does not comply with the formalities of a deed but does create a valid and enforceable contract between the parties to it.

Land law textbooks will almost always refer to the case of *Walsh v Lonsdale* in this regard.

KEY CASE ANALYSIS *Walsh v Lonsdale* (1882) 21 Ch D 9

Background

An agreement for lease was entered into but the lease was never executed. The agreement provided for rent to be payable in advance. The plaintiff went into possession of the property and actually paid rent in arrears. The defendant took action to recover rent arrears on the basis of the original agreement, claiming that the rent should have been paid in advance.

Decision

The Court of Appeal held that the plaintiff occupied under an equitable lease on the same terms as the original contract and was therefore in breach of that agreement by paying rent in arrears.

On the face of it the decision in *Walsh v Lonsdale* would suggest that there is no need to worry about the formalities required for the creation of a legal lease because an equitable lease will be created on the same terms. You should remember, however, the nature of equitable interests and their potential to bind third parties. If an equitable lease has been created out of an unregistered freehold title it would need to be protected as a Land Charge. An equitable lease is a form of estate contract (which we introduced in Chapter 4) and so requires registration as a C(iv) Land Charge in order for it to be binding on third parties. If the freehold title is registered then you will recall that in Chapter 3 we looked at the requirement for registration of a notice on the title registers to protect equitable interests and alert third parties to the existence of the interest. Failure to do this will mean that an equitable tenant in occupation of a property must rely on their interest being treated as an overriding interest of a person in actual occupation under Sch. 3 para. 2 of the Land Registration Act 2002.

PERIODIC TENANCIES

There is one more type of lease that we must consider, the periodic tenancy. This is a form of legal lease despite, on the face of it, contradicting the stated requirement for certainty of term when creating a leasehold estate in land. The nature of a periodic tenancy is that it continues indefinitely until it is brought to an end by notice. It is granted from period to period – in other words from week to week, month to month or year to year.

Periodic tenancies can be created expressly or impliedly. A landlord and tenant could agree to create a periodic tenancy that runs from month to month on payment of a monthly rent with the ability to bring the arrangement to an end on a month's notice, for example. This might offer the landlord and tenant the type of commercial flexibility mentioned at the beginning of this chapter.

Often, however, periodic tenancies will be implied where someone is in exclusive possession of a property and is paying rent but where the requirements for a valid lease have not otherwise been met. The case of *Prudential Assurance Co. Ltd v London Residuary Body* referred to at the start of this chapter is a good example of how a periodic tenancy operates. You will recall that a lease was granted until the land was required for road widening purposes and was therefore, on the face of it, void for lack of a certain term. However, the House of Lords found that, provided each period was itself certain, the effect was that the term would continue as though at the end of each period the parties had made a new agreement for a fresh term. Lord Templeman stated:

> A tenancy from year to year is saved from being uncertain because each party has power by notice to determine at the end of the year. The term continues until determined as if both parties made a new agreement at the end of each year for a new term for the ensuing year.

The period will be determined by reference to payment of rent, so a tenancy granted on the basis of a monthly rental payment will be a monthly periodic tenancy. Note, however, that a periodic tenancy is implied on the basis of the intention of the parties to create a lease. Where there is no intention there cannot be an implied tenancy. In *Javad v Mohammed Aqil* [1991] 1 WLR 1007 negotiations for the grant of a lease continued while the defendant was in occupation of premises paying rent. When those negotiations broke down the Court of Appeal decided that there had been no implied periodic tenancy but merely a permission to occupy while negotiations were proceeding.

SUMMARY

- A lease is both a contract and capable of existing as a legal estate in land.
- For a valid lease to exist there must be a term certain and exclusive possession. Periodic tenancies are not an exception to this rule but are treated as a series of terms certain, capable of being renewed at the end of each term for a new period.

- Leases granted for up to three years may be made orally. Leases for over three years must be made in the form of a deed.
- Leases granted for over seven years are required to be registered.

FURTHER READING

Bright, J., 'The Uncertainty of Certainty in Leases' (2012) LQR 128 – this is a useful article that summarises the law relating to certainty of duration but considers the possibility of reform as a result of the Supreme Court decision in *Mexfield Housing Co-operative Ltd v Berrisford* [2011] UKSC 52 (SC).

Dixon, M., *Modern Land Law*, 9th edn (Routledge, 2014) – refer to this textbook for a more detailed review of the law relating to leaseholds.

Government Departments website, Private renting for tenants: tenancy agreements: www.gov.uk/private-renting-tenancy-agreements/overview – this government website offers a basic overview to the public on what a tenancy agreement is and the terms that should be included.

The Leasehold Advisory Service, Living in Leasehold Flats: www.lease-advice.org/publications/documents/document.asp?item=7 – this is a government funded body that offers advice on entering into a lease and offers basic advice on key features of leaseholds as well as a guide to some of the terminology.

Warner-Reed, E., *Optimize Land Law*, 1st edn (Routledge, 2014) – this book has a useful summary of the key methods for termination of leases.

Chapter 7
Adverse possession

LEARNING OBJECTIVES

After reading this chapter, you should be able to:

- explain the meaning of adverse possession and its implications for ownership of land;
- identify the different ways in which adverse possession can arise;
- differentiate between the rules relating to adverse possession before and after the Land Registration Act 2002.

INTRODUCTION

You may begin reading this chapter with a preconceived idea of what adverse possession is all about. Many students will approach the topic from a perspective of their understanding of 'squatters' rights' and most reading this chapter will have come across the stories in the press about individuals claiming ownership of property on the basis of the fact that they have taken occupation when a property was vacant without the owner's consent.

In fact, although adverse possession can arise in those instances, the reality is that for the most part adverse possession is claimed in respect of much smaller parcels of land where the true ownership has become blurred and individuals have occupied and treated land as their own in the mistaken belief that they own rights in relation to that land.

Many claims for rights to land through adverse possession develop from shifting boundaries or lost title deeds and many are not controversial. Whether it is a derelict property or a strip of land at the back of a garden the rules that must be applied are the same and these will be covered in this chapter.

DEFINITIONS

Adverse possession is the occupation over a period of time of land belonging to a third party openly and without their consent which can, in certain circumstances, result in the occupier acquiring rights in relation to that land. It is sometimes referred to as 'dispossession of the paper title owner', in other words the true owner of the estate in land (demonstrated through their title) loses their rights in relation to the land in favour of the occupier.

On the face of it this sounds quite extreme. In effect, it sounds as though land can be stolen from the true owner. On the other hand, as we have identified earlier in this book, land is a finite and valuable resource and where it is abandoned or otherwise unused then it makes sense to have some means by which others can acquire and make effective use of it. Equally, with the ownership of land comes responsibility and so if an attempt is made to dispossess the true owner of their title then that owner should act to prevent this or otherwise risk losing their land. The rules that have developed around adverse possession are, therefore, an attempt to find a balance; to prevent the theft of land but find ways to allow efficient use of it where it would otherwise be impossible to do so.

THE TESTS TO BE APPLIED

As with the approach in the rest of this book we will break down the tests for determining whether there is adverse possession into stages. We will first consider the tests to determine whether the occupier has, in fact, gone into adverse possession of the property (which apply whether title to the land is registered or unregistered) and we will then look at the length of time that the occupation must have existed in order to determine that rights have been acquired. In the case of the latter we will have to look at the separate rules that apply to unregistered and registered land.

Is there adverse possession?

Not all occupation of land will lead to the potential for a claim of adverse possession. We have already come across a number of ways in which individuals might be said to have some degree of occupation rights. Tenants living in a house as a result of the grant of a lease are clearly in occupation of the property but could not be said to be in adverse possession because they are there with the consent of the landlord and subject to the terms of the lease. (Equally, guests who are invited for the weekend are there with your permission but are generally expected to leave at the end of the stay and are certainly not entitled to take up possession and claim rights over your home!) Easements may create rights that allow temporary access over a property but those rights are limited to the easement created. In all of those cases the rights and occupation are generally exercised with the consent of the estate owner and are limited in some way, whether by duration of the rights granted or the nature of the rights themselves. They are also all lesser rights, subject to someone who has a superior title and who has created or granted them.

There are a number of essential tests, then, that first have to be met to determine whether adverse possession is capable of existing. These include the requirements that the occupier has factual possession of the land, holds the necessary intention to possess and is in occupation without the consent of the true owner. We will cover each in turn.

On-the-spot question

? Having established that a lock-up garage has been abandoned and is sitting empty, a local entrepreneur decides to make use of the space and starts to store garden furniture in it with a view to selling it on the internet. They buy a padlock for it, come and go regularly with new stock and are never challenged about their use of it. Do they have a potential claim for adverse possession?

A number of cases have considered each of the requirements for adverse possession and we will briefly look at some of the facts of these.

Factual possession can be evidenced in different ways depending on the circumstances but the courts have tended to look for some demonstration of exclusive physical control of the land. In *Powell v McFarlane* (1979) 38 P&CR 452 it was said that the alleged possessor should have been '*dealing with the land as an occupying owner might have been expected to deal with it and that no one else has done so*'. In that case the occasional use of the land by a teenager to take hay and grass to feed a cow and on a few occasions organise a clay pigeon shoot was not sufficient evidence of factual possession. One way of demonstrating factual possession might be the fencing off of the land and in *Seddon v Smith* (1877) 36 LT 168 this was described as '*the strongest possible evidence of adverse possession*'. Enclosing land and dealing with it as an owning occupier might do sends a strong signal of factual possession. In *Buckinghamshire CC v Moran* [1990] Ch 623 a landowner annexed neighbouring land belonging to the county council to his own and eventually a lock and chain were added which meant that the land could only be accessed from the landowner's land. This enclosure was enough to evidence exclusive control over the land and therefore factual possession. The occupier does not need to be continually present and use of land for grazing cattle and storing timber have both satisfied the courts that factual possession was present. The occupation does, however, have to be open. In other words, if the occupation is concealed so that the paper owner is unaware of the position and therefore unable to take action it is likely that it will be held that there is no adverse possession. The courts have also identified that 'trivial' acts will not be enough to constitute adverse possession. So, in the case of *Tecbild Ltd v Chamberlain* (1969) 20 P&CR 633 the fact that children had played and exercised their ponies on the land claimed was not sufficient.

Intention to possess is potentially more difficult to evidence. There is some degree of overlap with the former test but factual possession alone will not suffice. Interestingly, this test does not require the claimant to evidence an intention to *own* the land – simply to possess it. A good illustration of this comes from the leading authority of *Pye v Graham*. This case, which eventually reached the Grand Chamber of the European Court of Human Rights in 2005, and its facts and decisions provide a very useful insight into the development of the law in this area.

KEY CASE ANALYSIS: *Pye (JA) (Oxford) Ltd v Graham* [2002] UKHL 30

Background

Pye were the owners of the legal title to the land and in 1983 gave consent to the Grahams to occupy the land, on payment of a licence fee. From 1984 the Grahams continued to occupy the land without the permission of Pye (and apart from one payment in 1984 without paying Pye any further money). They remained willing, however, to pay for the use of the land. In 1997 the Grahams registered a caution at the Land Registry (effectively giving notice to Pye that they now claimed the land as theirs).

Decision

It did not matter that the Grahams had offered to pay to use the land. A squatter needs only to demonstrate an intention to possess the land and not necessarily to own it.

In *Pye v Graham*, Lord Browne-Wilkinson examined the requirement for intention as well as factual possession and offered a useful example that helps to explain the difference between the two. He commented that an individual in occupation of a locked house could be a squatter but could equally be an overnight trespasser or even a friend looking after the house while the owner is on holiday. In each case there is factual possession of the house but only the squatter has the necessary *intention* to possess. He also considered that if a squatter was in possession of the land and a stranger entered onto the land that entry would be a trespass against the possession of the squatter – whether or not the squatter intended in the long term to acquire title. In other words what you are looking for is an intention to exercise physical control of the land for your own benefit: an intention to exclude all others including the paper owner. In that sense the evidence may be similar to that of factual possession, so the annexation of land as in the *Buckinghamshire CC v Moran* case sends a message that the occupier is in control of that land to the exclusion of all others – even the true estate owner.

Finally, there must be an absence of consent from the title owner. This is more straightforward. In the Pye case, for example, the period during which the Grahams held under licence and paid a licence fee could clearly not constitute adverse possession because they were there with the consent of the true owners. Once the licence had expired and the Grahams openly continued their occupation of the land, treating it as though it were their own and excluding all others, including Pye, adverse possession began.

On-the-spot question

At the end of a fixed term tenancy agreement the tenant fails to vacate the property. They request a new tenancy and the freehold owners agree to this in principle but subject to the renegotiation of the terms. The freehold owners tell the tenant that they are willing to allow them to remain in the property while the terms are negotiated but that if a new tenancy is not agreed they expect the tenant to vacate. Is the tenant in adverse possession of the property?

Once it is established that there is evidence of adverse possession of land we then need to consider the ways in which a claim can be brought by the occupier. In some cases land could be occupied for many years without either the paper owner or occupier taking any action to regulate the position. However, often there will be an event that triggers a requirement for a claim for adverse possession, for example if one or other of the parties decides to sell the land in question and issues are then raised on the title.

The way in which a claim is made will depend on whether title to the land is registered or unregistered and whether the Land Registration Act 2002 applies.

CLAIMING TITLE THROUGH ADVERSE POSSESSION – UNREGISTERED LAND AND THE LIMITATION ACT 1980

The Limitation Act 1980 applies where title to the occupied land is unregistered. Importantly it also applies to registered land where the occupier has acquired rights through adverse possession prior to the coming into force of the Land Registration Act 2002. Although the amount of unregistered land is diminishing, it is important still to understand the rules here. As we have said, adverse possession arises in relation to small parcels of land where ownership is unclear or title deeds have been lost and there is no record of registration at the Land Registry. In these cases the Limitation Act 1980 will be applied.

It is helpful to think of the operation of the Limitation Act as a ticking clock that is, over a period of time, eroding the rights of the paper owner in favour of the adverse possessor. s.15(1) of the Act provides that:

> No action shall be brought by any person to recover any land after the expiration of 12 years from the date on which the right of action accrued to him or, if it first accrued to some person through whom he claims, to that person.

This means that the person seeking to recover the land (which may be the paper owner or, indeed, anyone else with a superior title to the occupier) must act within the 12-year period to seek to remove the occupier or risk losing their title. This links back to the comments made earlier in the chapter that with land ownership comes responsibility as well as rights and an owner must take positive action to remove a squatter or risk losing those rights.

s.15(1) refers to the 'date on which the right of action accrued' and this date needs to be identified in order for the clock to start ticking. The right of action to recover the land begins on the date on which the owner is dispossessed or they discontinue their use of the land and the adverse possessor takes possession.

On-the-spot question

 Think about the case of *Pye v Graham*. At what point do you think that the Grahams dispossessed Pye of the land and when did the clock therefore start ticking under the Limitation Act 1980?

Once the clock starts ticking the adverse possession must be continuous. If at any point the paper owner retakes possession then the clock will stop and will start again from the beginning if and when there is a subsequent dispossession. It will also stop if there is an acknowledgment of the superior title of the paper owner by the squatter. So, for example, if someone in adverse possession writes to the paper owner asking them, as the owner of the land, to consider selling the land to them, that is likely to constitute an acknowledgment that stops the clock (although, interestingly it would appear that an oral offer to purchase would not constitute acknowledgement). If, following the letter, the owner takes no action to regulate the position either through a sale of the land, lease or licence and the occupier remains in possession, then it is possible that the clock will start running again.

Importantly, though, provided the adverse possession is continuous it can comprise occupation by more than one person; in other words there can be successive occupation by different 'squatters' that, when added together will constitute the required 12-year period of adverse possession resulting in the owner losing title. There must be continuity –

so any break in the chain of occupation where the land lies vacant until a subsequent squatter takes possession might stop the clock running. Interestingly, subsequent squatters on the land also risk a challenge to their possession not only from the paper owner but also from their predecessors in adverse possession of the land. So a squatter who is dispossessed by another squatter can exercise rights against the new squatter until such point as the Limitation Act prevents them from doing so.

On-the-spot question

A piece of land (title to which is unregistered) purchased by a house builder in 1982 and for which planning permission was never obtained to build lies disused until 1995. At that point a local farmer moves onto the land, erects fencing and a padlocked gate and starts to graze sheep on the land. The farmer dies in 2001 and six months later a neighbouring equestrian centre takes over the land and builds stables on it. In 2008 the house builder writes to the equestrian centre informing them that they intend to take possession of the land. Who, in your view, has the better claim to the land?

The effect of an uninterrupted period of adverse possession that satisfies the requirements of the Limitation Act 1980 is not automatically to transfer legal title to the squatter. In the first instance they will acquire an equitable title, which can be converted to a legal title by registration. The equitable interest that is acquired is an overriding interest; providing the squatter is in actual occupation it will be binding on third parties. For a reminder of the overriding interests of those in actual occupation have a look back at Chapter 3. On registration, normal practice is for the Land Registry to grant a possessory title in the first instance, which can then subsequently be upgraded to an absolute title after 12 years of registration.

One final point to bear in mind is that the Limitation Act 1980 will also apply to claims for adverse possession made in respect of registered land where the 12 year period of adverse possession was completed before the coming into force of the Land Registration Act 2002.

CLAIMING TITLE THROUGH ADVERSE POSSESSION – REGISTERED LAND AND THE LAND REGISTRATION ACT 2002

The rules relating to claims of adverse possession were changed by the Land Registration Act, which now determines the procedures for making claims in relation to registered land where the period of adverse possession is completed after the coming into force of the Act (which, you will recall, was on 13 October 2003). The changes were, in part, a response to the fact that in unregistered land it was possible after the requisite period to automatically defeat the paper owner's title and call for registration of the land. As we suggested earlier in the chapter, it was often the case that in relation to unregistered land the claim for adverse possession came about because the title deeds were lost or there was some other ambiguity about ownership. This could not be the case, however, in relation to registered land where the public facing and transparent registers of title give a clear indication as to ownership and rights in relation to the land. That title cannot, on the face of it, be defeated and the ability to acquire title automatically through adverse possession under the Limitation Act 1980 seemed to sit in direct contradiction to this key principle of land registration.

The new rules are set out in Schedule 6 of the Act. The key differences to the rules that we covered in relation to the Limitation Act 1980 earlier in the chapter are that the 12 year period for adverse possession is reduced to 10 years but at the end of that 10 year period there is no automatic entitlement to title to the land. Instead an application must be made by the occupier to the Land Registry requesting registration. Crucially, at that point the Land Registry will contact the registered proprietor of the land asking them whether they would seek to oppose the application. This is an important additional step in the process that alerts the registered proprietor to the claim that is being made and allows them an opportunity to take action to prevent it. Remember that in relation to unregistered title it was possible for landowners to 'sleep' on their rights and as the clock ticked on if they failed to act positively to retake possession of their land they risked losing it altogether. The effect of the Land Registration Act is to prevent this from happening and to offer the registered proprietor the opportunity to take action.

If, having served notice on the registered proprietor, they fail to respond then the squatter will automatically be registered in place of the original owner.

If the registered proprietor *does* respond to the notice and objects to the application then the squatter's application will be rejected unless one of the following conditions (set out in Schedule 6 to the Land Registration Act 2002) applies:

- it would be unconscionable because of an equity by estoppel for the registered proprietor to seek to dispossess the squatter and the circumstances are such that the squatter ought to be registered as the proprietor;
- that the squatter is for some other reason entitled to be registered as the proprietor;
- that the squatter has been in adverse possession of land adjacent to their own for at least 10 years under the mistaken but reasonable belief that they are the owner of it.

These three conditions require a little explanation. The first sounds complicated but the principle is quite straightforward. It relates to the equitable doctrine of proprietary estoppel that protects individuals who are given assurances by landowners on which they rely and incur expenditure. An introduction to the doctrine of proprietary estoppel is contained in the Beginning Equity and Trusts book in this series. In essence, proprietary estoppel might apply in relation to adverse possession where the registered proprietor of the land had encouraged in some way the person in occupation to believe that they actually owned the land and that the person in occupation had acted on that belief (perhaps investing money in the redevelopment of the land for example). In that case it would be wrong for the registered proprietor to then act to defeat a claim by the occupier for title. It would be for the squatter to provide evidence that this had happened.

The second condition is much broader and would cover a variety of other reasons and offer greater discretion in determining whether the squatter should be entitled to registration. The Law Commission (in their report 'Land registration for the twenty-first century, a conveyancing revolution') gives as an example a situation where the squatter has entered into a contract to buy the land, has paid a purchase price to acquire the land and has moved into occupation of the land but has never actually been registered as the proprietor. In that situation, although the squatter may not have acquired a legal title they have almost certainly acquired equitable rights in relation to the property that ought to entitle them to complete their registration as legal owner.

The final condition is potentially likely to be the most common ground on which a squatter may rely. The condition links back to comments made at the beginning of the chapter where we discussed the ways in which adverse possession may arise. This condition is likely to arise where boundary structures have shifted over the years or were originally put up in the wrong place and as a result the position on the ground does not match the title plans. It is worth remembering that it is quite rare for Land Registry plans to fix the boundaries exactly (remember that in Chapter 3 we looked at the registers of title and the general boundaries that are delineated on the title plan). It is, therefore, often difficult to define the exact extent of the legal boundary. The owner is under the honest misapprehension that they are the owner of both their own title and the additional adjoining land. Often this misapprehension does not come to light until the point at which they decide to sell their land and enquiries and investigations are made into the extent of their title.

If none of the conditions apply then the registered proprietor's counter notice will have been successful. However, this is not necessarily the end of the story. It does not, of course, automatically follow that if the registered proprietor is successful the squatter will immediately vacate the land and further legal action may be required in order to gain possession from the squatter. If this action is not taken and the squatter is allowed to remain in occupation of the land the Land Registration Act will allow them to reapply to be registered as proprietor after a further two years have elapsed since the first application was rejected. If this happens the squatter will automatically be successful and registered as proprietor without the opportunity for the registered owner to oppose it.

ADVERSE POSSESSION AND HUMAN RIGHTS

The decision of the House of Lords in the *Pye v Graham* case resulted in Pye losing title to valuable land to the Grahams. The case was taken to the European Court of Human Rights where Pye sought compensation for the loss from the UK government on the basis that the law of adverse possession was inconsistent with the rights under the European Convention for the Protection of Human Rights for individuals to peacefully enjoy their possessions without interference from the state. In 2005 the Court of Human Rights found that the Limitation Act 1980 did breach the Convention rights as Pye had been deprived of its land without warning or compensation. This fundamental challenge to the laws of adverse possession eventually ended up at the highest European Court, the Grand Chamber where the decision was that there was no breach, the limitation periods set out by the Act being a balance between extinguishing a title at the end of the period and allowing the owner to take action to prevent this from happening.

SQUATTERS' RIGHTS – A FINAL WORD

There have been some recent changes in the law that might result in a reduction of claims for adverse possession in relation to residential buildings. From 1 September 2012 it became illegal under the Legal Aid, Sentencing and Punishment of Offenders Act 2012 to squat in residential buildings; this can now lead to six months in prison, a £5,000 fine or both. The new law applies both to squatters in occupation after the coming into effect of the Act but also to those who were already in occupation. The law has prompted some debate about whether criminal trespass will preclude claims for adverse possession (on the basis that a person should not be able to acquire rights on the basis of criminal acts). However, a recent High Court decision in *Best v The Chief Land Registrar* [2014] EWHC 1370 (Admin), confirmed that this would not be the case. We will have to wait to see whether the new law reduces the number of claims of adverse possession in respect of residential properties.

SUMMARY

- Adverse possession is a means of acquiring title to land as a consequence of occupation of land over the requisite period of time. It is often referred to as 'dispossession of the paper title owner', confirming that the true owner loses all rights in favour of the squatter.
- The basis of any claim for adverse possession is that the squatter has factual possession of the land and an intention to possess and has been in occupation openly and without the consent of the landowner for the requisite period.

- The Limitation Act 1980 covers unregistered land and provides that the right to recover the land is lost 12 years after adverse possession first begins.
- The Land Registration Act 2002 covers registered land and removes the automatic award of title, replacing it with notice to the superior title owner to act once the squatter has been in occupation for 10 years.

FURTHER READING

Colby, A., 'No Adverse Reaction' (2014) *The Estates Gazette*, p. 95 – this article reviews a 2014 test case (*Best v Chief Land Registrar* [2014] EWHC 1370 (Admin)) on whether the new criminal offence of squatting in residential buildings effects the law on adverse possession.

Dixon, M., *Modern Land Law*, 9th edn (Routledge, 2014) – refer to this textbook for a more detailed review of the law relating to adverse possession.

Land Registry Practice Guide 5 – *Adverse possession of unregistered land*: www.landregistry. gov.uk/professional/guides/practice-guide-5 – this useful online guide sets out the Land Registry's approach to applications for adverse possession but also contains a useful summary of the key requirements.

Land Registry Practice Guide 4 – *Adverse possession of registered land*: www.landregistry. gov.uk/professional/guides/practice-guide-4 – this useful online guide sets out the Land Registry's approach to applications for adverse possession but also contains a useful summary of the key requirements.

Land Registry Practice Guide 42, *Upgrading Possessory Titles to Absolute Titles*: www.land registry.gov.uk/professional/guides/practice-guide-42-upgrading-the-class-of-title – this practice guide will give you more information about what happens when an application is made to upgrade a title from possessory to absolute.

Chapter 8
Easements

After reading this chapter, you should be able to:

- recognise and appreciate the easement as an important interest in land;
- distinguish between common types of easements;
- identify the tests commonly used to establish whether a right is capable of existing as an easement;
- compare and contrast the different means by which easements may be created;
- select the appropriate means of protecting an easement, depending on whether the land has a registered or unregistered title.

INTRODUCTION

There is no hiding from the fact that the law relating to easements is complex. The Law Commission recommends a 'simplification and rationalisation' of the law in this area in its report 'Making land work; easements, covenants and profits à prendre' presented to Parliament in 2011. At its most basic level the nature of an easement as an interest in land is not difficult to appreciate. As will become apparent, we come across easements of one type or another all the time – often without even realising it. The difficulty arises when it comes to considering the variety of ways in which easements can be created and particularly in relation to easements that are implied or that are acquired through the ancient law of prescription. This chapter aims to break down some of these concepts, explaining some of the key legal terms and giving you the foundation from which to build with your land law studies.

Closely linked to the topic of easements is the law relating to profits à prendres. These are commonly described as rights to take something from another's land. The suggested reading at the end of this chapter will allow you to explore these rights further but we do not focus on them here.

WHAT IS AN EASEMENT?

On-the-spot question

? I live in a terraced property. When I take my bins out every Monday evening I have to use a pathway that runs across the back gardens of my neighbours' properties and then connects with an alleyway that leads to a gated access onto the main road. On what basis do you think I am entitled to use the pathway and alleyway to get out onto the street?

Perhaps surprisingly there is no legal definition of an easement. As a consequence, easements are commonly explained and described by the use of examples, which is the approach we will take here.

Most of us will recognise that when we walk down the high street or drive to the shops we are allowed to do so as members of the public because the footpaths and highways are designated for public use and the law allows us rights to use them. We do not have to ask for permission to do this and, indeed, most of us will exercise these rights without thinking twice about them. Imagine, on the other hand, that we are interested in buying a house on a small private development, where the access to houses is via a private road leading off the public highway, perhaps with a sign indicating that the access is not a public right of way but is for the use of residents and their guests only. Based on what you have already learned about land law this should raise questions in your mind. Who owns that private road (in other words who has the title to the land), who has the rights to use it and on what basis? The answer lies within the law relating to easements. In the example given the ownership of the private road might lie with the developer who originally acquired the land and has built the houses or, more commonly, with the owners of the houses that front the road. Often a management company will take a transfer of the title to the road and will accept responsibility for its maintenance. The owners of the houses will often hold shares in the management company and will make financial contributions towards its upkeep.

The rights to use the private road are then 'given' to the owners of the houses. We would normally refer to this as a right of way over the road. In legal terms what has been created is an easement – a right of one landowner (the owner of the house) to use land that is in the ownership of another (the private driveway owned by the management company).

The right of way is probably the most common and most easily understood of the category of interests known as easements but there are lots of other examples of rights that can exist as easements and many of these will be mentioned in this chapter.

On-the-spot question

 Can you think of a time when you might have exercised a right over someone else's land that might qualify as an easement?

The first thing we must consider is *when* a right is capable of existing as an easement. The right of way we have referred to is an obvious example but what about others? This will be the focus of the first part of this chapter.

The question you might then ask is *how* are these rights created? We need rules and procedures to work out whether and how an easement has been acquired by a landowner. In the example we have used it is very likely that when the developer first sold the houses on the private development the purchasers were given these rights expressly. This chapter will explain how this is done in legal terms. More complicated, however, is a position where a landowner is claiming an easement but has no documentary evidence to show that the right (whatever it might be) was expressly given. The law relating to easements has created a complex set of means by which easements can be created by implication or by long use. This chapter will break down these methods, dealing with each in turn and explaining how they operate.

The last thing we will consider is to what extent easements will bind successors in title to the land. In other words if one of the purchasers on the private development, having been expressly given an easement to use the private road, were to sell their property, would the buyer of that house automatically acquire the benefit of the right of way? The nature of the easement as a property right and its potential to benefit and bind others will conclude this chapter (Figure 8.1).

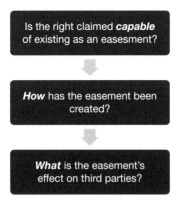

Figure 8.1 A suggested structure for approaching the law relating to easements

WHEN IS A RIGHT CAPABLE OF BEING AN EASEMENT?

In a structured approach to learning the law relating to easements a sensible place to start is to consider whether or not a particular right claimed is capable of existing as an easement. If the answer to that question is 'no', then there is no sense in moving forward to consider the ways in which the right may have been created.

In order to determine whether or not a right is capable of existing as an easement we must introduce the key case of *Re Ellenborough Park* [1956] Ch 131.

KEY CASE ANALYSIS – *Re Ellenborough Park* [1956] Ch131

Background

The Court of Appeal was asked to consider the nature of a right that had been granted in relation to a communal garden area in the middle of a square surrounded by houses.

Decision

The Court of Appeal decided that the right to use the communal garden could exist as an easement, but more importantly laid down the criteria that must be met for a valid easement to exist. These are:

- there must be a dominant and servient tenement;
- the easement must accommodate the dominant tenement;
- the dominant and servient tenements must be in separate ownership;
- the easement must be capable of forming the subject matter of a grant.

The tests that came from *Re Ellenborough Park* will need to be applied to the right claimed in order to determine whether the right is capable of existing as an easement.

Key definitions

Tenement: land.

Dominant tenement: the land that benefits from the easement.

Servient tenement: the land that carries the burden of the easement.

There must be a dominant and servient tenement

Although in the context of easements we talk about individuals having rights over land owned by others, this requirement provides that for an easement to exist there must be *land* that is capable of benefitting from the right and *land* that carries the burden of it. Easements are attached to the land itself and do not belong to the individual. For example, if pipes that carry the foul drainage from a property cross the land of another before emptying into a public sewer the third party land under which the drains run carries the burden and the land on which the house stands (from which the pipes run) is the land which benefits. The former is the servient tenement and the latter is the dominant tenement. In the first example given in this chapter, the houses fronting the access road on the private development would be dominant tenements and the road itself is the servient tenement. It is crucial to the success of a claim for an easement that there are separate pieces of land. Offering a trainee solicitor friend from the city an open invitation to visit and enjoy walks across the fields adjacent to your country home is unlikely to meet this requirement. A right granted for the personal benefit of an individual, therefore, would fail this test.

The easement must accommodate the dominant tenement

This second criterion is an extension of the first. The easement must benefit the land to which it is attached and not just the owner of that land. A classic example of this comes from the case of *Hill v Tupper* (1863) 2 H&C 121 (159 ER 151).

KEY CASE ANALYSIS: *Hill v Tupper* (1863) 2 H&C 121 (159 ER 151)

Background

Hill was granted a lease of land adjacent to a canal. The lease granted Hill an exclusive right to put pleasure boats onto the canal. Tupper started putting his own pleasure boats on the canal. Hill sued Tupper claiming an easement granting him a right to put his boats onto the canal which Tupper had interfered with.

Decision

The court held that the right did not accommodate the land leased to Hill but rather was a right that benefitted Hill's business rather than the land itself and was not, therefore, an easement.

This criterion also requires there to be sufficient proximity between the dominant and servient tenements. Even if the friend from the city referred to above owned a house that was capable of being a dominant tenement the easement would likely fail because it cannot be seen to benefit the land itself but rather the individual, i.e. the friend who was given the permission. This is particularly the case where the properties are some distance apart. The dominant and servient tenements do not have to be adjacent to each other but there must be sufficient proximity.

The dominant and servient tenements must be in separate ownership

This requirement is, on the face of it, relatively straightforward. Since the very essence of an easement is that one landowner exercises rights over another landowner's land, it stands to reason that the tenements are in separate ownership. There are, however, some significant consequences of this requirement and proposals for reform offered by the Law Commission. These can be accessed through the further reading suggested at the end of this chapter.

The easement must be capable of forming the subject matter of a grant

> ### Key definition: Deed of grant
>
> A legal document that complies with the requirements of a deed that expressly grants an easement over land.

This requirement often causes confusion among students because of the terminology used. The express creation of a legal easement requires that the formalities of a deed are used. Deeds that grant new easements to landowners are called 'deeds of grant'. In essence this criterion requires that the easement claimed must have been capable of being granted through a deed. It is perhaps best understood as a means for the courts to retain control over the range of easements that might be granted. Where a right granted by deed has previously been accepted by the courts as one of a recognised group of interests capable of existing as easements, then it is capable of forming the subject matter of a grant. A right of way is an obvious example. Where there is no precedent it does not necessarily mean that the right cannot exist – but rather that the courts will have to decide whether it can be added to the list. There are a number of subsidiary requirements that help to clarify whether an easement meets this criterion but these are outside the scope of this book.

THE CREATION OF EASEMENTS

Easements can be created in a number of ways. The flowchart in Figure 8.2 depicts the three broad means by which easements can be created and then breaks them down into subcategories. We shall work through each in turn.

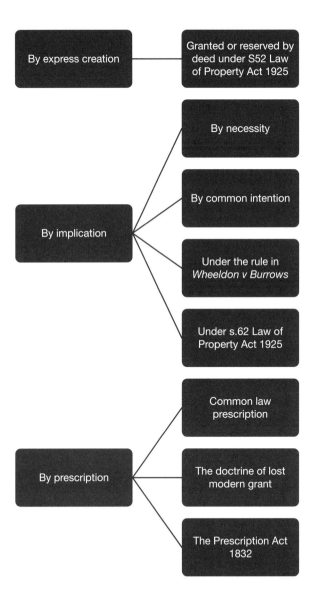

Figure 8.2 A summary of the basic ways in which easements can be created

EXPRESS CREATION OF EASEMENTS

As a lawyer instructed to act for clients purchasing a new property being constructed on a residential development, part of your role would be to consider those easements that would be required in order that your clients could better enjoy their new property. Access over private roads, the ability to use shared driveways, the passage of foul water through pipes leading from the kitchen or bathroom, the drainage of rainwater into surface water sewers – all are issues that might require the consideration of whether there are easements already in existence or whether new easements need to be created.

Having established what rights your clients might need, your next job would be to ensure that these were drafted appropriately into a legal deed that complies with the relevant formalities. More often than not this document will be the transfer deed used to transfer title to the property into your clients' names. Done in this way the easements will have been expressly created, following negotiation and agreement between the owners of the dominant and servient tenements.

On-the-spot question

 Can you remember what the formalities for the creation of a deed are?

Easements granted and reserved

In the example given above the clients buying the new property need to be *given* easements in order to fully enjoy the use of their new home. Easements that are given in this way are referred to as easements *granted*. In other words, if I sell a piece of land and grant that land (the dominant tenement) rights over the land I retain (the servient tenement also known as 'retained land') I am *granting* an easement.

Easements are also capable of being reserved. If a landowner decides to sell off part of their garden to a developer who wants to build a private access road over it into a new development in the process of construction, the landowner might want to retain a right of way for themselves over that access road once it is completed. This would be an easement that is *reserved*. A reserved easement is therefore a right that is retained over land that is sold. In other words, if I sell a piece of land (the servient land) and reserve over it a right of way benefitting the land that I retain (the dominant land), I am reserving an easement.

The reasons why it is important to be able to distinguish between easements that are granted or reserved will become apparent in the next section dealing with implied easements.

IMPLIED EASEMENTS

While many easements are created expressly through deeds of grant or reservation, a great number also arise impliedly in a variety of ways. It is important to appreciate that easements created in this way carry no less weight than expressly created easements. Where an easement has been created in this way it is *implied* that the easement was created by deed and so satisfies the formalities.

The difficulty with implied easements is that the methods by which they are created are varied and, at times, complex. As with other aspects of land law the best way to approach them is to break them down into manageable concepts.

Easements of necessity

The principle here is relatively straightforward. These easements are implied where the right is essential for the use of the land. So, for example, where a seller disposes of land and the buyer's only means of access to the public highway is across the seller's privately owned retained land then an easement of necessity may be implied. This would be an implied grant of an easement but the rule applies equally to an easement that would have been reserved. This easement derives from the assumption that the parties must have intended that there would be an easement because without it the land sold (or indeed retained) could not be used. Note, though, that the right must be *essential*. In other words, just because a right might make the use of the land more convenient does not mean that an easement of necessity will be implied.

On-the-spot question

 If, on the sale of land, the seller expressly provides that no easements will be granted and the buyer subsequently discovers that the land is landlocked will an easement be implied?

Easements of common intention

There is some degree of overlap here with easements of necessity and students sometimes confuse the two. They are, however, distinct categories of implied easements and easements of common intention have a wider scope than easements of necessity. Easements of common intention intervene to give effect to the use for which the land was transferred. As with easements of necessity the right must be *essential* to enable the owner of the benefitted land to use the land as was intended. Again, this category of easements applies to easements both granted and reserved.

KEY CASE ANALYSIS: *Wong v Beaumont Property Trust* [1965] 1 QB 173

Background

The dominant tenement was leased to a tenant to use as a restaurant, with a requirement in the lease that 'all noxious smells' should be eliminated.

Decision

The Court of Appeal confirmed the decision of the earlier courts that an easement had been implied allowing the tenant to erect a ventilation shaft on the landlord's property in order to comply with the requirement and so use the kitchens in the restaurant as was intended.

The rule in *Wheeldon v Burrows*

The case of *Wheeldon v Burrows* introduced a concept known as *quasi easements*. In order to understand the rule it is helpful to first understand how quasi easements operate. They are founded on the notion that when land is owned by one common owner, that owner exercises rights in respect of the land that would be classified as easements if, in fact, the land were in separate ownership.

Imagine, for example, that a landowner builds two cottages, A and B, on his property that share an access to the public highway. The electricity cables that connect to both properties run underneath land adjacent to cottage B and are shown by the broken line in Figure 8.3.

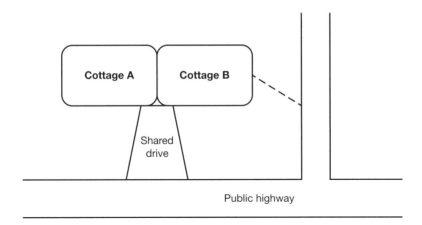

Figure 8.3 A diagram to help explain the rule in *Wheeldon v Burrows*

When the land is in common ownership the owner will use the shared drive for the benefit of both cottages and will run services through the cables to bring electricity to the properties. There is no requirement for easements because the land is owned by one person who clearly has the right to occupy and use the property (subject to certain limitations) as they wish. However, the law recognises that the owner is exercising *quasi easements*. It might help to think of these as almost imaginary easements, rights that the owner is exercising in respect of their own land. If the owner were then to sell Cottage A to a third party, the rule in *Wheeldon v Burrows* would potentially operate to turn those quasi easements into real easements, impliedly granting to the owner of Cottage A the right to use that part of the shared driveway that runs across the land retained by Cottage B and the right to use the electricity cables running underneath the land at Cottage B.

There are conditions that have to be met before *Wheeldon v Burrows* will apply. These are:

- immediately prior to the transfer of land the quasi easement must have been used for the benefit of the dominant land;
- the quasi easement must be 'continuous and apparent';
- the quasi easement must be necessary for the reasonable enjoyment of the dominant land.

The rule in *Wheeldon v Burrows* is a useful means of implying easements where there has been a failure to deal with this adequately in the transfer deed relating to the sale. However, there is one significant limitation to the rule and that is that it applies only to easements granted and not reserved. Many standard forms of conveyancing contracts address this by expressly extending the rule to both grants and reservations.

On-the-spot question

? A landowner disposes of part of their land to a local farmer who intends to graze cattle on it. Prior to the sale the landowner used the field as a shortcut to get to the local village shops. In the transfer deed no mention of any such right was made. When the landowner tries to exercise the right subsequent to the sale the farmer tells him he is trespassing. Has the landowner acquired any rights under *Wheeldon v Burrows*?

s.62 Law of Property Act 1925

The rule in *Wheeldon v Burrows* and s.62 of the Law of Property Act 1925 are often referred to together and do bear many similarities but they operate in quite different ways. s.62 is a word saving provision, designed to ensure that on the transfer of land existing easements and rights will automatically be transferred also. It often comes as a surprise to students to learn that it has also been used by courts to facilitate the creation of new easements.

The reason for this lies in the wording of s.62 which states that on a conveyance (whether by sale or lease) of land there shall be 'deemed' to be included 'all . . . liberties, privileges, . . . rights, and advantages whatsoever' relating to and enjoyed by the land. The effect of s.62 is to turn these rights, which may have previously been enjoyed in a quite informal way, into easements once the land is transferred.

The effect of s.62 might be best explained by reference to the authority of *Wright v Macadam*.

KEY CASE ANALYSIS: *Wright v Macadam* [1949] KB 744

Background

A tenant held a lease of a top floor flat and during the lease term was allowed by the landlord to store coal in the coal shed that was located in the garden area. The lease expired and a new lease was granted with no mention of any right to use the coal shed. The landlord subsequently demanded payment for its use.

Decision

The Court of Appeal held that there had been implied into the new lease an easement giving the tenant the right to use the coal shed. The earlier permission that had been given had been elevated by s.62 into a full blown easement.

Strictly speaking, easements created under s.62 are not implied and require no intention or necessity. They come about because s.62 deems the rights to have been expressly included in the conveyance. We deal with them here, however, because there is some overlap between the idea of quasi easements discussed in relation to *Wheeldon v Burrows* and the way in which easements are created under s.62. There are however, some basic differences set out in Table 8.1.

Table 8.1 Differences between the rule in Wheeldon v Burrows and s. 62

Wheeldon v Burrows	s.62 Law of Property Act 1925
Applies when what become the dominant and servient tenements are originally in common ownership	Applies where there has been diversity of ownership of the dominant and servient tenements
The right must be 'continuous and apparent'	No requirement for 'continuous and apparent' right
Both legal and equitable easements can be created	Only legal easements pass under s.62

The Law Commission has proposed that the current methods of implying easements be replaced with one statutory principle that easements will be implied 'where they are necessary for the reasonable use of the land at the time of the transaction (unless the parties have expressly excluded its operation)'. What is 'reasonable' will be determined by five factors. The explanation of the current law and the proposals for reform by the Law Commission is a very useful resource for students.

EASEMENTS BY PRESCRIPTION

In its most basic form the law relating to prescription simply provides that if a right is exercised for long enough, openly, peacefully and without the permission of the landowner, it will eventually become an easement. The concept is similar to that of adverse possession where occupation of land over a number of years may give rise to ownership rights in favour of the occupier.

Imagine, for example, that an individual has for many years used a path over his neighbour's land as a means of accessing his allotment. The principle of prescription means that provided the individual has exercised this right for the requisite period, quite openly, without ever asking the permission of the landowner and without using force, he may have acquired an easement of way over the land.

However, although the concept is relatively straightforward, unfortunately the law in this area is complex. The main reason for this is because a number of different methods for acquiring rights through prescription have developed. When considering whether a right might have been acquired by long use of land each of the methods must be considered when deciding on the merits of a claim.

Common law prescription

In order to acquire an easement under the common law rules you are required to show that a right has been exercised 'since time immemorial', defined by statute as being since 1189. The difficulties in demonstrating this should be obvious! However, in practice the claimant must show that the right has been exercised for at least 20 years and on that basis it is *presumed* to have been exercised since time immemorial. On the face of it common law prescription looks relatively straightforward. However, the presumption of prescription can be rebutted on evidence that the right could not have existed in 1189 or came into being subsequent to that date. In many cases this evidence will be relatively easy to find.

Doctrine of lost modern grant

As an alternative to common law prescription the doctrine of lost modern grant was developed to allow prescription to operate where there was evidence of at least 20 years' use but without the need to go back to 1189. The principle behind the doctrine is that courts will assume that a deed was executed in modern times granting the right but that the deed was subsequently lost – hence the 'lost modern grant'. It is only possible to rebut this presumption by demonstrating that during the period when the grant could have been made there was no one capable of making the grant.

Statutory prescription

The third method of acquiring rights through prescription is under the Prescription Act 1832. The Act introduced two periods for prescription: 20 years and 40 years. While there remain limited circumstances where a claim for 20 years may be defeated, a claim for 40 years shall according to the Act 'be deemed absolute and indefeasible'. This, on the face of it, is relatively straightforward but there are additional requirements set out by the Act in relation to the periods for which the right is claimed, including that the right must have been continuous and 'uninterrupted' and that the right must have been enjoyed for the required period immediately prior to the proceedings through which the right is claimed.

The fact that there are three methods by which prescription may be claimed makes the law in this area, in the view of the Law Commission, unnecessarily complicated and there is a proposal that the current law be abolished and a new statutory scheme set up for the creation of easements through prescription.

THE NATURE OF AN EASEMENT AS A PROPERTY RIGHT

It is important to recognise that not all rights granted will qualify as easements. If a landowner decides to allow their neighbour to walk across their property as a shortcut to the public highway there are a number of ways in which this could be achieved. At one end of the spectrum a full blown easement in the form of a right of way could be granted. At the other end the landowner might offer a simple verbal consent allowing permission. The former, if effectively granted, will be of benefit not only to the neighbour but to anyone who buys the neighbour's property. The latter, which suggests the creation of a licence, is very unlikely to benefit anyone other than the neighbour for the time being and may be withdrawn at any time.

An easement, if created effectively, is capable of being a legal interest in the land. This is the effect of s.1(2)(a) of the Law of Property Act 1925. As we have seen, an expressly created easement must be made in the form of a deed but, in order to be legal, it must also be registered where the servient tenement has a registered title. Failure to register will mean that the easement cannot exist at law but is an equitable interest, which itself must be protected by registration of a notice. Failure to do this would mean that the easement would not be binding on a purchaser of the servient tenement. The position in relation to implied easements is slightly different. By their very nature it is unlikely that these easements would have been registered but they are potentially still binding on purchasers of the servient tenement as overriding interests. This category of interests was discussed in Chapter 3.

EXTINGUISHMENT OF EASEMENTS

The last thing to consider in relation to easements is the ways in which easements can be brought to an end. A dominant landowner may expressly release an easement by execution of a deed. Similarly, if the dominant and servient tenements come into common ownership, easements as between the two will cease to exist (remember that one of the essential characteristics of an easement is the separation of the dominant and servient tenements). Finally, it is possible that a dominant landowner might 'abandon' their easement through non-use. Proving abandonment, however, is not straightforward.

SUMMARY

- Easements are property rights that are capable of existing as legal interests in land.
- In order to exist as an easement, a right has to satisfy the characteristics of easements as set out in the case of *Re Ellenborough Park*.
- Once a right is identified as being *capable* of existing as an easement, the methods of creation must then be considered.
- Easements can be created expressly, impliedly or through prescription.
- Expressly created legal easements over registered land must be protected by registration.

FURTHER READING

Dixon, M., *Modern Land Law*, 9th edn (Routledge, 2014) – refer to this textbook for a more advanced exploration of the issues raised in this chapter.

The Law Commission, 'Making land work: easements, covenants and profits à prendre' (Law Com No 327) – this report was written to propose changes to the current law on easements but also contains useful background reading on the development of the law in this area. You can access an online version on the companion website.

The Land Registry, Training Programme on Easements – this free online training is actually designed for practitioners but offers a very useful background to the law of easements with some good examples. You can access the online training on the companion website.

Chapter 9
Freehold covenants

LEARNING OBJECTIVES

After reading this chapter, you should be able to:

- understand the importance and relevance of covenants in relation to land law and the conveyancing process;
- appreciate the difference between positive and restrictive covenants;
- recognise the different rules that apply under common law and equity;
- explain why and how the Law Commission is proposing changes to the law relating to covenants.

INTRODUCTION

As with the topic of easements, the basic principles of the law of freehold covenants are relatively straightforward but there are complexities in this area that are often confusing both to students new to the topic and even to more experienced practitioners. This is in part the reason why the Law Commission has called for reform in this area.

The key to understanding freehold covenants is to structure your approach to learning the law in this area and to break down the concepts into manageable chunks. The aim of this chapter is to introduce you to the key concepts and law in a structured way to offer you the foundations in this topic on which to build with further reading and study.

We will start by looking at the nature of a covenant as a contractual promise relating to land between the parties who create it and will then consider the position of those parties who subsequently acquire the land after the covenant has been made. This will require us to think about a number of different rules arising out of the application of the common law and equity.

It is important to remember that this chapter deals with an introduction to *freehold* covenants. The law relating to leasehold covenants is different in some fundamental respects. A detailed consideration of leasehold covenants is outside the scope of this book but the suggested reading at the end of the chapter will support your further study in this area.

WHAT IS A COVENANT?

On-the-spot question

? You are in the process of buying a brand new house on a local housing development. The site office tells you that in order to keep up the appearance of the development there will be a number of obligations imposed on you as a buyer. These include obligations to contribute towards the maintenance of a driveway shared with your neighbours, to maintain the fencing along the boundary, not to park a caravan on the front driveway and not to use the house for business purposes. How do you think that the developers will ensure that these obligations are met by both you and the other buyers of houses on the development?

In essence, a covenant is a form of contract. Technically it is a contract made in the form of a deed and so requires the rules for the creation of a deed that we saw in Chapter 2 to be met in order to create it. Remember that to be valid a deed must comply with s.2 of the Law of Property (Miscellaneous Provisions) Act 1989 and must also state on its face that it is a deed, be executed appropriately and be delivered. Most new covenants will be created in the transfer document entered into when land is disposed of or through a separate deed of covenant.

A covenant is also a contractual promise either *to* do or *not* to do something in relation to land and is often also referred to as a promise made in the form of a deed. The parties to that deed are referred to as the covenantor and covenantee and it is important as a student of land law to appreciate the difference between the two for reasons that will become apparent.

Key definitions

Covenantor: the person who makes the promise.

Covenantee: the person to whom the promise is made.

Wherever there is a covenant there is also a burden and corresponding benefit in relation to the land. As you would expect, the covenantee, to whom the promise is made, will take the benefit of the covenant and the covenantor, who makes the promise, will take the burden.

Finally, the nature of a covenant is that it can be positive or negative/restrictive. A promise to do something, for example to build a boundary structure, is positive in nature. It requires positive action in order to comply and often involves some form of expenditure. The person who gives that covenant (the covenantor) takes on the burden of compliance – in other words by building the boundary structure.

A promise *not* to do something is, therefore, negative or restrictive in substance. A covenant that provides that the covenantor will *not* build on their property does not, on the face of it, require positive action. It restricts what the landowner can do with their property and is complied with by simply not building.

These two examples are straightforward but it is important to look at the substance of a covenant before deciding whether it is positive or restrictive. A covenant not to allow a hedgerow to grow above a certain height, for example, looks on the face of it to be restrictive because it is drafted in the negative. However, the substance of the covenant is actually positive because it requires positive action in order to comply. Covenants are often drafted by lawyers in the negative for reasons that will be explained as you work through this chapter but it is important to remember to always look beyond the wording at the substance before deciding whether a covenant is positive or restrictive.

On-the-spot question

 A buyer of a new house covenants with the developer who is selling not to allow the exterior of the property to fall into disrepair. What is the nature of the covenant entered into?

COVENANTS AS CONTRACTUAL OBLIGATIONS

The basic common law principle of privity of contract provides that only the parties to a contract can enforce the terms of that contract against each other. A more detailed discussion of the doctrine of privity of contract is included in Chapter 8 of *Beginning Contract Law*, which sets out the general rule but also a number of important exceptions (two of which we will mention below).

In Chapter 2 we used the example of Hathaway Farm to illustrate how rights might be created in relation to land. In that example the owners of Hathaway Farm had sold a cottage on their land to a third party. The diagram used is reproduced in part in Figure 9.1.

Imagine that on the sale of Hathaway Cottage the owners of the farm were keen to ensure that the cottage should only be used as a private residence, that the boundary fence should be maintained by the new owners and that nothing should be built on the land without the prior written consent of the owners of the farm. These obligations are all capable of existing as covenants and could have been drafted into the transfer deed that conveyed title to the buyers of the cottage.

In the Hathaway Farm example the owners of the cottage would be the covenantors and the owners of the farm the covenantees. They would also be the original parties to the contract and so if the new owners of the cottage were to breach the covenants that they had entered into, for example by building a new detached garage on the land without consent, they could be pursued for breach of contract by the owners of the farm in the usual way.

The position becomes more complex, however, if and when one of the original contracting parties were to sell their land. Imagine that five years after acquiring the cottage the owners decided to sell up and move on. The person that buys the cottage from them subsequently starts up a business from the cottage and has a constant stream of customers visiting them at the property. He fails to maintain the boundary fence line which becomes dilapidated and is an eyesore to the owner of the farm. Can the owners of the farm enforce the covenants that were originally entered into when the cottage was sold against the new owner of the cottage, notwithstanding the fact that he was not a party to the original contract and there is no privity of contract between them?

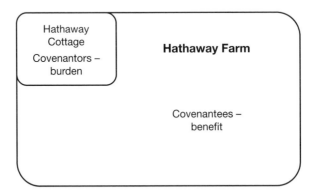

Figure 9.1 Re-visiting Hathaway Farm in the context of covenants

THE RUNNING OF COVENANTS WITH THE LAND

The basic principle of privity of contract would suggest that, whenever land that is either burdened or benefitted by covenants is sold, the successors in title to the original contracting parties will not be entitled to take on the burden or benefit of those covenants because they were not party to the original contract.

Key definition: Successor in title

A person deriving their title from a previous owner of the property. For example if X sells their property to Y and transfers their title in the property to them, Y becomes a successor in title to X.

There are a number of statutory exceptions to this rule, one of the most important of which is the Contracts (Rights of Third Parties) Act 1999. An explanation of the changes that the Act made to the principle of privity of contract is contained in *Beginning Contract Law*. While the Act has made it possible for the benefit of a covenant to pass to a third party it is subject to the original covenant being drafted in such a way as to make it clear that the benefit is for a third party who is either identified in the contract or is *identifiable* as a member of a class or answering a particular description in the contract. This, together with the fact that the Act only applies to the passing of a benefit and only to contracts entered into after 11 May 2000 means that in many cases this statutory exception will not apply.

Property law does, however, in certain circumstances allow for the running of covenants with the land. In other words the benefit or burden is allowed to pass to successors in title. Unfortunately, the rules that allow for the running of covenants are a mixture of common law and equitable rules and each needs to be considered in turn. It is at this point that the law relating to covenants becomes much more complicated and getting to grips with it requires us to look at each aspect in turn. Figure 9.2 suggests a structure for approaching this.

The running of the burden of covenants at common law

We will start with the most straightforward of the rules. At common law, whether the covenant is positive or restrictive, the burden will not run with the land. This rule was confirmed as long ago as 1885 in *Austerberry v Corporation of Oldham* (1885) 29 Ch D 750 and more recently in *Rhone v Stephens* (1994) 2 AC 310.

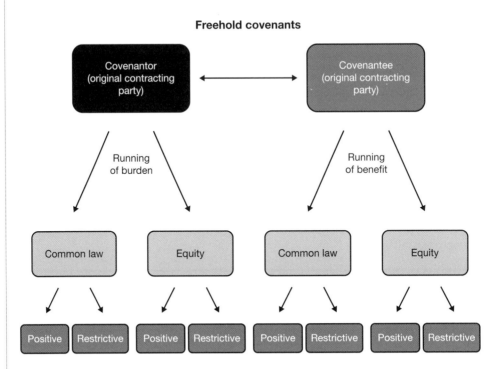

Figure 9.2 A suggested structure for dealing with the law relating to covenants

The effect of this in relation to our example of Hathaway Cottage is that when the original convenantors sell the cottage the buyers will not, in common law at least, acquire the burden of the various covenants that were originally given. It is worth noting at this point that this does not mean that the covenants simply disappear. By virtue of the doctrine of privity of contract, the original cottage owners remain liable for the covenants, notwithstanding that they have sold the property. This could potentially create problems for original covenantors who can remain liable for breaches of covenant by their successors in title long after they have parted with possession of the property.

The running of the burden of covenants in equity

Equity is often described as mitigating the harshness of the common law rules and the law relating to covenants is no exception. In the nineteenth century one of the most well-known cases in land law found a means of allowing the burden of certain covenants to run in relation to a very popular part of London, Leicester Square.

KEY CASE ANALYSIS: *Tulk v Moxhay* [1848] 2 Ph 774

Background

In 1808 Mr Tulk sold land in London to Mr Elms. Elms covenanted 'for himself, his heirs and assigns' that he would 'at all times thereafter at his own cost keep and maintain the piece of ground in sufficient and proper repair, in an open state, uncovered with any buildings, in neat and ornamental order'. There was a mixture of positive and restrictive obligations – effectively to maintain and repair and not to build on the land. Mr Tulk retained land that was benefitted by this covenant. By 1848, ownership of Leicester Square had passed to Mr Moxhay, who wanted to build there. An injunction was granted to restrain such a breach of covenant.

Decision

A covenant may run with the land in equity provided:

1   the covenant is restrictive (negative) in substance;
2   the covenant was intended to benefit land retained by the covenantee;
3   the burden of the covenant was intended to run with the land of the covenantor;
4   the person against whom the covenant is being enforced has notice of it.

The rule in *Tulk v Moxhay* is well known and still holds true today. It requires a little further explanation. First, it only applies to covenants that are restrictive in substance. It does not, therefore, affect the position in relation to positive covenants where the principle remains that the burden will not run.

Second, there must be land retained by the covenantee that is capable of benefitting from the covenant. You will recall that when we looked at easements in Chapter 8 there was a requirement for dominant and servient land. The same principles apply in relation to covenants. Where there is a burden there has to be a corresponding benefit that attaches to definable land. There is an important exception to this rule – that of a building scheme. This will be discussed later in the chapter.

Third, the burden of the covenant must be intended to run. There is statutory help here in the form of s.79(1) of the Law of Property Act 1925, the effect of which is to assume that the burden will run unless expressed to the contrary.

Finally, the purchaser of the land must have notice of the covenant. In other words the covenant must be protected by registration. We looked at the protection of restrictive covenants by registered notices in Chapter 3 and as D(ii) Land Charges in Chapter 4. Failure to protect a restrictive covenant in this way will result in the burden not running with the land.

On-the-spot question

? A local authority sells land to a residential developer subject to a covenant not to build anything on the land other than single storey dwellinghouses. One of the houses that the developer constructs is sold to an architect who wants to build a second storey on the house. What are the implications of the covenant that was originally entered into by the developer?

If we relate this back to our Hathaway Cottage scenario the result is that the owners of Hathaway Farm (and original covenantees) would potentially be able to pursue the new owner of Hathaway Cottage for the breach of covenant against using the property as anything other than a private dwellinghouse. This covenant is restrictive in substance and provided the other tests in *Tulk v Moxhay* have been satisfied, is enforceable against the new owner.

The running of the burden of covenants – conclusions

Equity has, therefore, softened the effects of the common law but only in certain situations. The basic principles are that the burden of a positive covenant will not run with the land either at common law or in equity. The burden of a restrictive covenant will not run at common law but will, subject to the rule in *Tulk v Moxhay*, run in equity.

This partly explains why, as mentioned earlier in the chapter, solicitors have tended to draft covenants in the negative. Other mechanisms have also developed to protect original covenantors who remain liable under privity of contract and to facilitate the transfer of the burden of covenants. The most important of these is the chain of indemnity covenants. On the sale of property by the original covenantor they will seek to extract an indemnity, (essentially a promise to compensate financially if the seller is sued for breach of covenant) from the buyer, protecting themselves against future breaches. When the buyer then sells they will also take an indemnity covenant and so on. The result is that a chain of these indemnity covenants is created. If the original covenantor is then pursued for a breach of the covenant by one of their successors in title they will enforce the indemnity down the chain to the person who is in breach. The theory is sound but in practice any break in the chain of indemnities will effectively make them worthless and it is often difficult if not impossible to locate the original covenantor to start with.

It is also worth remembering that these rules relate to the transmission of freehold covenants. The rules in relation to leasehold covenants are much more straightforward and it is accepted law that the burden of landlord and tenant covenants will run. This is the effect of the Landlord and Tenant (Covenants) Act 1995.

One final exception to the rule that the burden of a positive covenant will not run is the limited rule that comes from the case of *Halsall v Brizell* [1957] Ch 169. In this case the courts found that buyers of houses on an estate that benefitted from shared rights to use driveways and sewers should also accept the corresponding burden of contributing towards their upkeep (a positive covenant). This rule has a very limited (but potentially important) application.

On-the-spot question

The owner of a house on a modern estate claimed that she should not be subject to the positive covenants to contribute towards the cost of maintenance of the private road within the estate because she did not drive and did not therefore derive any benefit from the right of way over the road. She was not the original buyer of the house, having acquired the property from them only recently. Is she bound by the covenant to contribute?

The running of the benefit of covenants at common law

Having considered the running of the burden of covenants we now turn to the running of the benefit. As before we have to consider the different approaches of common law and equity.

At common law the benefit of a covenant, whether positive or restrictive will only run if the following tests (explained in more detail below) are met:

1   the covenant touches and concerns the benefited land;
2   at the date of the covenant, the original covenantee held a legal estate in the land;
3   the successor in title derives their title from or under the original covenantee;
4   at the date of covenant, the benefit must have been intended to 'run with' the land.

The case of *P & A Swift Investments v Combined English Stores Group* [1989] AC 632 offered a test for establishing whether a covenant 'touches and concerns' the land. This requires that the covenant benefits the *owner* of the land only for as long as they own it and would cease to be of benefit if it were separated from the land. In other words it attaches to the land itself and not to the owner. The covenant must also affect the nature, quality, mode of use or value of the benefitted land. Importantly, even if the other tests are satisfied the covenant will not touch and concern if it is expressed to be for the personal benefit of the covenantee.

The ownership of the legal estate in the land by the covenantee should be a relatively straightforward concept to you now, as is the successor in title acquiring their title from the original covenantee (or a successor in title to the original covenantee). In relation to the last of the tests to allow the benefit of a covenant to run, s.78(1) of the Law of Property Act 1925 assumes that the intention is for the benefit to run (in much the same way as s.79 of the same Act does in terms of the running of the burden).

The rules relating to the running of the benefit of covenants at common law are, then, relatively straightforward. However, the scope of application of these rules is actually quite narrow. Where a successor in title to the original covenantee is trying to enforce the benefit of covenants against the original covenantor then these rules will apply. However, we have established that as soon as the original covenantor disposes of *their* interest the only way that the burden of covenants will run is in equity (and then only if they are restrictive in substance). In that case the corresponding running of the benefit will also need to be dealt with using equitable principles. In other words, if you are applying equitable principles to one half of the equation then you must apply equitable principles to the other half as well.

The running of the benefit of covenants in equity

The running of the benefit of covenants in equity again becomes more complex because there are three methods through which this can happen. They are through annexation, assignment or a building scheme. We will deal with each, briefly, in turn. First, however, a requirement that is common to all three methods, is that the covenant must 'touch and concern' the benefitted land. This is a concept that we have already covered and will not be repeated here.

Annexation

Annexation, as the name would suggest, relates to the attachment of the covenant to the land. Writers often refer to this as a 'nailing' of the covenant to the land. Once attached, the benefit will be transferred to successors in title. There are three ways in which annexation can occur: expressly, impliedly and by statute. Express annexation will occur where the wording of the covenant is such as to make it clear that there is an intention that the benefit should attach to and run with the land. As you might expect there have been a number of cases where decisions have turned on the nature of the drafting used to annex the benefit of the covenants. For that reason you will often come across covenants that have been drafted on the basis that they benefit land retained by the covenantee '*and each and every part thereof*' – a direct attempt by lawyers to ensure that *all* of the land capable of benefitting is, in fact, benefitted.

Implied annexation has a much more narrow application and requires the courts to be able to infer annexation by the relevant circumstances and conduct of the parties. This is rarely relied on in practice and we mention it here only for the sake of completeness.

Statutory annexation requires us to return to s.78(1) of the Law of Property Act 1925 which has been interpreted broadly by the courts in recent years to allow the benefit of covenants to be annexed to each and every part of the benefitted land.

KEY CASE ANALYSIS: *Federated Homes Ltd v Mill Lodge Properties Ltd* **[1980] 1 WLR 594**

Background

Land with the benefit of planning permission to build houses was divided into parcels, one of which was sold to Mill Lodge, subject to a restrictive covenant relating to the numbers of houses that could be built on the site. The remaining parcels of land were eventually sold to Federated Homes without provision for the express annexation of the benefit of the covenant entered into by Mill Lodge. The Court of Appeal had to decide whether the effect of s.78(1) Law of Property Act 1925 served to annex the benefit of the covenant to the land.

Decision

The effect of s.78(1) is such that provided the covenant touches and concerns the land it will operate to annex the covenant to the land allowing it to run with the land and benefit successors in title.

The broad interpretation of s.78(1) in the Federated Homes case has been criticised. On the face of it, provided a covenant touches and concerns the land, there is no longer any need to demonstrate either express or implied annexation because s.78(1) will create a statutory presumption of annexation. Subsequent cases have confirmed that courts will look at all of the circumstances of the case – so that if there is clear evidence of a contrary intention (for example that the covenants were for the personal benefit of the covenantee only) then s.78(1) will not apply.

Assignment

The assignment of the benefit of a covenant can take place on a transfer of that land provided that it is possible to identify the land that it is intended to benefit and that the benefit of the covenant is assigned at the time of the transfer (in other words it is part of the overall transaction rather than taking place separately, at another time). While there might appear, on the face of it, to be similarities between annexation and assignment, the latter relates to a transfer of the benefit to a person (i.e. the buyer of the land) rather than attaching to the land itself and therefore on each sale there is a requirement for a fresh assignment.

Building scheme

The final way of running the benefit of a covenant in equity is through a building scheme. In order to understand the nature of a building scheme it is useful to stop and consider the nature of the running of covenants on a typical housing development.

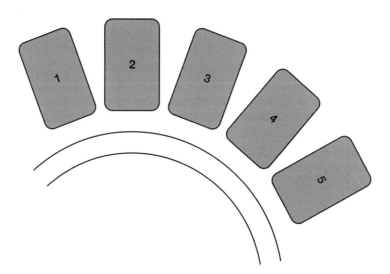

Figure 9.3 The running of covenants in a typical housing development

Imagine that the houses in Figure 9.3 are all new, built on a housing development owned by one housebuilder. The housebuilder wants to impose on the buyers a covenant that they will not use the houses as anything other than private dwellings. The houses are sold in order so that when No 1 is sold the buyers become original covenantors, the developer is covenantee and No 1 has the burden of the covenant while the remaining land belonging to the developer (including Nos 2 to 5) has the benefit. When No 2 is sold it takes on the burden of the covenant and the remaining land still belonging to the developer (now including only Nos 3 to 5 because No 1 has already been sold) takes on the benefit. If you follow this process through you will quickly realise that when No 5 is sold last of all it will take on the burden but none of the other houses will take on the benefit because they have all previously been sold and therefore did not acquire the benefit on subsequent sales by the developer. The implication is, then, that if No 5 were to breach the covenant and start to operate a bed and breakfast from the property, on the face of it, none of the other house owners can enforce the covenant against them.

The creation of a building scheme will enable owners of property within the scheme to enforce the covenants against all other owners within the scheme and to enable all others to enforce covenants against them, avoiding the problem outlined above. The requirements for a building scheme come from the case of *Elliston v Reacher* [1908] 2 Ch 374:

1   The claimant and defendant must have both purchased their land from the same seller.
2   The seller must have created a scheme of development, in other words divided the land into plots as part of a planned arrangement.
3   There must have been an intention that the covenants would be mutually enforceable between original buyers of the plots and their successors in title.
4   The buyers bought the plots in the knowledge of the scheme.

One further requirement is that the building scheme must relate to a defined area of land.

More recently the courts have adopted some flexibility in their approach to these requirements, treating them more as guidelines rather than strict tests that have to be applied. The result, where a building scheme is found, is to create a set of mutually enforceable covenants that are of benefit and burden to all owners of property within the scheme.

The running of the benefit of covenants – conclusions

There is clearly much more opportunity for the benefit of covenants to run with the land when compared against the running of the burden. It is possible for the benefit to run at both common law and in equity and through a variety of means. You will need to understand the different ways in which the benefit can run but also how to apply the rules to different situations.

POTENTIAL REFORM OF THE LAW RELATING TO COVENANTS

As with the law relating to easements, the Law Commission has recommended simplifying the law relating to covenants in its report 'Making land work; easements, covenants and profits à prendre'. This includes a proposal to introduce a new way of making obligations attach to the land (by creating new interests called 'land obligations') and enabling positive as well as restrictive covenants to be enforceable against successors in title. Once original contracting parties have sold their land they will no longer be liable for the land obligations, so removing the difficulties that the principle of privity of contract causes on disposals and the need for artificial means of passing on obligations, such as chains of indemnity covenants to exist. This would, no doubt, be a relief to both practitioners and law students alike!

SUMMARY

- Covenants are obligations relating to land that are contractual in nature and can be positive or restrictive in substance.
- The principle of privity of contract means that original parties to the creation of a covenant remain liable on that covenant even after they have disposed of the land.
- Whether and how covenants can run with the land and benefit or burden successors in title to the original parties depends on the nature of the covenant and the application of common law and equitable rules.
- The law relating to covenants is subject to criticism and there are proposals for fundamental reform of this area of property law.

FURTHER READING

Dixon, M., *Modern Land Law*, 9th edn (Routledge, 2014) – this textbook will provide you with further information on the law relating to leasehold covenants.

The Law Commission, *Privity of Contract: Contracts for the Benefit of Third Parties* (Law Com No 242, 1996) – this report looks at the need for reform of the law relating to privity of contract.

The Law Commission, *Making Land Work: Easements, Covenants and Profits à Prendre* (Law Com No 327, 2011) – this report was written to propose changes to the current law on covenants but also contains useful background reading on the development of the law in this area. You can access an online version on the companion website.

The Land Registry, *Practice Guide 72 – Development Scheme* – to find out more about how the Land Registry deals with schemes of development have a look at their useful practice guide. You can access the guide on the companion website.

Martin, J., 'Remedies for breach of restrictive covenants' (1996) 329–341 *The Conveyancer and Property Lawyer* – this is a useful article to read if you want to find out more about the remedies that the courts can impose for breach of restrictive covenants.

O'Connor, P., 'Careful what you wish for: positive freehold covenants' (2011, 3) 191–207 *The Conveyancer and Property Lawyer* – this is an interesting alternative view to the proposals for reform of positive covenants.

Chapter 10
Mortgages

LEARNING OBJECTIVES

After reading this chapter, you should be able to:

- appreciate some of the history behind the development of the law relating to mortgages;
- explain how the rights of the borrower are protected;
- explain how the rights of the lender are protected and the remedies that they have if a borrower defaults;
- understand how priorities of mortgages operates;
- demonstrate an awareness of different types of mortgage and their place in the conveyancing process.

INTRODUCTION

Most of us will come across mortgages in one form or another at some point during our lives. If we aspire to own property then the likelihood is that we will only be able to buy that property by borrowing the money to allow us to do it. Taking out a mortgage will be part of the conveyancing transaction that we enter into.

The mechanics of taking out a mortgage, understanding the terms and conditions associated with it and the conveyancing practice that determines the procedures that are followed are generally more likely to be part of study on a postgraduate legal practice course. However, we will touch on them briefly in this chapter because it helps to make sense of the academic legal principles that govern the law relating to mortgages and the ways in which those rules have developed.

We will start by defining what a mortgage is, the law that relates to them and protection for borrowers and lenders, and will then look at the remedies available when the terms of a mortgage are breached.

WHAT IS A MORTGAGE?

A mortgage is an example of a proprietary right in relation to land. We introduced the concept of proprietary rights in Chapter 2. Remember that a proprietary right attaches itself to the land rather than being personal to the owner for the time being of that land. This creates an important distinction between mortgages and other forms of money lending. A temporary personal loan is often referred to as a non-secured loan. In other words, the arrangement between lender and borrower is a personal, contractual one. A mortgage, however, while still a form of contract, creates security for the loan in the form of the property itself. The consequences of this mean that if the debt is not repaid on the agreed terms the lender may be able to exercise remedies that will ultimately allow them to take possession of the property. This is what is commonly, but strictly speaking inaccurately, referred to as a repossession.

On-the-spot question

 You arrange a personal loan with your bank and use the money to do some home improvements, including a small conservatory on the back of the house. What rights do you think the bank would have if you failed to make your repayments?

Importantly, though, unlike other proprietary interests that endure in relation to the land (restrictive covenants or easements for example), a mortgage is time limited and where the borrower has complied with the terms of their mortgage (by repaying the debt in full, for example) then the mortgage will cease and the proprietary interest that was held will be extinguished.

In this chapter we will refer to the parties to a mortgage as the lender and borrower. In other reading you may come across references to the mortgagee and mortgagor.

Key definitions

Mortgagee: the lender, the person, bank, building society etc. with the benefit of the mortgage who holds the security.

Mortgagor: the borrower, the person who has the liability under the mortgage.

We will start by looking at the historic development of the mortgage and will then look at this interest as a modern phenomenon and the rights and obligations that it creates.

DEVELOPMENT OF THE MORTGAGE

The concept of a mortgage has been around for hundreds of years. Historically, when a mortgage was created the fee simple (remember that this is the freehold estate) was actually transferred to the lender as part of the arrangement. When we talk today about lenders effectively owning our houses when we have large mortgages in place over them – this was actually the case!

The transfer of the property was subject to a right of redemption. This provided that where, by a given date (called the legal redemption date), the debt plus any interest was repaid in full to the lender, there was a requirement on the lender to re-convey the property to the borrowers. As we will see shortly we still talk about the legal right to redeem a mortgage today but in the modern world this has a slightly different meaning.

Key definition: Legal right of redemption

The right of the borrower to reclaim their property on repayment of the mortgage debt.

Provided the debt was repaid by the date set for redemption, the mortgage was discharged and the ownership returned to the borrower. If, however, repayment was not made by the due date then the consequences were severe. The lender simply retained the ownership of the property and the borrower lost all of their rights and had no further recourse against them. Historically, this was the case even where the value of the property exceeded the debt due.

As we have seen before in the development of land law, equity subsequently intervened to soften the harshness of the rules in relation to repayment of the mortgage debt and recognised the right of the borrower to redeem their mortgage by paying the debt even after the legal date for redemption had passed. This became known as the equitable right to redeem.

The legislation of 1925 changed the principle that when a mortgage was created the legal estate in the land was transferred to the lender. It recognised that the real owner of the property was the buyer and that what the lender had acquired was a proprietary interest in the land rather than ownership itself. This effectively enabled the conveyancing practice that takes place today to develop. In the majority of cases today the mortgage debt is repaid out of the money received when a house is sold. This was not possible where the ownership of the house vested with the lender. The law, therefore, developed to allow the borrower to retain the legal ownership and the lender to acquire a different form of interest.

Initially, the interest that was granted to the lender when a legal mortgage was created was either a long lease (in fact a *very* long lease of 3,000 years!) or a charge by way of legal mortgage. As with the transfer of the fee simple estate, the long lease was subject to a right of redemption in favour of the borrower and it came to an end when the debt was repaid. The legal date for redemption was six months after the mortgage was created, but in reality that date was meaningless. Once that date had expired, the equitable right to redeem took over.

The creation of a long lease by way of security for the mortgage no longer applies and we are now left with only one mechanism for protecting the interest of the lender under a mortgage – the legal charge. We will look at how this interest in the land is protected shortly. The significance of the distinction between legal and equitable dates for redemption has also diminished, although you will generally still find a legal date for redemption in most mortgage deeds and this date becomes relevant when the lender is seeking to enforce remedies against the borrower (which will be covered later in the chapter).

CREATION AND PROTECTION OF A LEGAL CHARGE

As we saw in Chapter 2, rules have to be followed where legal interests in land are created. The legal charge that protects a mortgage is no exception. A legal charge is required to be made in the form of a deed (the requirements for which are set out in Chapter 2).

Failure to use the correct formalities does not necessarily render the mortgage void but may result in an equitable mortgage being created. However, even in this instance the formalities for a contract under s.2 of the Law of Property (Miscellaneous Provisions) Act 1989 must be followed. Without them equity will not intervene.

In registered land the legal charge is then protected by registration in the Charges Register. There are examples of the registrations made in the sample Land Registry registers in Chapter 3 on registered land. If you look at those registers you will see that numbered entries 3, 4, 5 and 6 all relate to mortgages in relation to the property. There are two mortgages in that example, the lenders being Weyford Building Society and Fast and Furious Building Society. We will look at the position where there is more than one mortgage in relation to the property (and that takes priority over the other) shortly. In unregistered land the legal charge is protected by depositing the title deeds to the property with the lender. Bear in mind, however, that the occasions when this will happen now are greatly reduced, as the creation of a legal charge by way of mortgage both on the sale of unregistered land and even when created independently will trigger a registration of the land (and thus a registration of the legal charge in the Charges Register).

THE RIGHTS OF THE BORROWER

Equity's protection of the right to redeem

We have already introduced the key right in favour of a borrower under a mortgage – that of the right of redemption. This right has been in place since mortgages were first created and is as important today as it was then. The intervention of equity also means that, even if the legal date for redemption has expired, equity will protect the borrower and extend the right to redeem beyond that date.

It therefore follows that the right to redeem cannot be excluded or restricted. You will often see this referred to as 'clogs on the equitable right to redeem'. Terms of the mortgage deed that attempt to do this may be struck out by the courts.

KEY CASE ANALYSIS: *Fairclough v Swan Brewery Co Ltd* [1912] AC 565

Background

A mortgaged hotel was owned under a long lease. At the point at which the mortgage was created there were 17 years left to run on the lease. However, the mortgage deed restricted the right to redeem the mortgage until six weeks before the lease was due to expire.

Decision

The term restricting the right to redeem was held to be void. By the time the right to redeem came around the lease would be practically worthless because it would be so close to expiry.

It is worth noting, however, that in deciding whether the right to redeem has been restricted the courts will give due attention to the relative bargaining powers of the parties to the mortgage. Where an arrangement has been negotiated and a commercial agreement reached between parties and there is no evidence of oppressive bargaining power, then the courts may uphold the mortgage terms. This was the case in *Knightsbridge Estates Trust Ltd v Byrne* [1939] Ch 441 where a term of the mortgage deed effectively postponed the redemption date for 40 years but the term was held to be valid. The parties to the mortgage deed were commercially aware and had both received legal advice.

Borrowers are also protected from mortgage terms that are held to be oppressive or unconscionable. Again, consideration will be given to the nature of the parties to the arrangement so that someone without commercial awareness who enters into an arrangement subject to a term that is unreasonable may be protected, but where both sides to the bargain are experienced and hold equal bargaining positions the agreement may be upheld. For example, in *Cityland and Property (Holdings) Ltd v Dabrah* [1968] Ch 166 the loan arrangements required the borrower to pay a large premium on top of the capital borrowed, which equated to an interest rate of 57 per cent, which was held to be 'unfair and unconscionable'.

Finally, mortgage terms that give collateral advantage to the lender have also been carefully scrutinised by the courts. The effect of collateral advantage is to give to the lender some other benefit, as well as the standard rate of interest charged. Many of the cases where collateral advantage has been considered relate to 'tied' arrangements with breweries where, for example, the brewery might extend credit to its tenant running a pub or hotel on the basis that the tenant will only obtain its alcoholic drinks from that brewery. As with the other examples, the courts will look at the context of each case and the relative bargaining power before deciding whether the arrangement is unconscionable.

On-the-spot question

A first time buyer, concerned that they will not meet the stringent lending requirements of the high street lenders, is offered a mortgage by a wealthy distant uncle. The terms of that mortgage require the borrower to pay a standard rate of interest but also to transfer to the uncle a half share in the mortgaged property. The borrower is unsure as to whether this is appropriate but enters into the mortgage arrangement. Several years later the debt is repaid but the uncle refuses to transfer back the half share. Does the borrower have any rights?

Undue influence

We have considered a position where the terms of a mortgage arrangement are unfair or restrictive to the borrower. Undue influence relates to a position where, in themselves, the terms of a mortgage arrangement may be reasonable, but someone else (i.e. other than the lender) puts pressure on a borrower to enter into the arrangement when it might not otherwise be in their interests to do so.

The cases around undue influence usually involve family members or friends putting pressure on a borrower to take up a mortgage. The outcome of a number of high profile cases has encouraged a fundamental review of lending practices of the big high street lenders.

Imagine a situation where a husband and wife co-own property that is not mortgaged. The husband, without the knowledge of his wife, has run up large debts in relation to his business and needs to borrow money to repay these debts or risk losing his business. He negotiates a deal to borrow money from a lender who requires security for the debt in the form of a mortgage over the house. In order to create the mortgage both the husband and wife need to sign the mortgage deed because they are co-owners. The husband exerts pressure over his wife, perhaps telling her that this is the only option or misrepresenting the figure that is being borrowed. The wife signs the mortgage deed, without having obtained legal advice. Subsequently, the husband's business folds, the mortgage repayments are not met and the lender seeks to enforce their security by taking possession of the house. Is the wife able to claim that the pressure that was exerted on her to sign the mortgage deed without proper explanation or advice in relation to the liability means that the lender is unable to enforce their rights against her?

Similar facts were presented in the case of *Barclays Bank v O'Brien* [1994] 1 AC 180 where the House of Lords found that there had been undue influence and the mortgage was, therefore, unenforceable against the wife. They found that the bank had not taken appropriate steps to ensure that the wife had made an informed decision about signing the mortgage deed. The outcome of this case sent shockwaves around the legal profession at the time and prompted a review of the steps taken by lenders in ensuring that all parties to the mortgage were fully advised and informed. Subsequently, further guidance was provided as a consequence of the case of *Royal Bank of Scotland Plc v Etridge* (No 2) [2001] 3 WLR 1021 where the House of Lords examined the advice that should be given, which includes independent legal advice given by a solicitor.

THE RIGHTS OF THE LENDER

It is unlikely, given the recent difficult economic times, that you will have escaped news in relation to mortgage lending, interest rates and repossessions of properties across the country. Adverts for secured loans come with a warning that your property may be repossessed if you do not keep up with repayments. Following the housing boom that came to an abrupt end in 2007 many homeowners found themselves in a position where they had extended themselves with high loan to value mortgages and making those repayments became a struggle.

In legal terms, however, the term repossession is a misnomer because as we have seen the lenders never had possession of the property in the first place but rather an interest that, in certain circumstances, allows them to *take* possession of the property as one of a collection of remedies that is available to them. We will look at some of those remedies in this section.

The mortgage as a contract

The first thing to remember is that the mortgage is a contract between the lender and borrower and as a consequence normal contractual remedies will apply if one of the terms of that mortgage is breached. The most obvious way in which the contract might be breached is through non-payment of the debt that is due on the terms that were agreed. However, the same remedy applies for any breach of the contractual term so a mortgage term that prohibited use of the property as anything other than a private dwellinghouse, for example, might result in legal action if it transpires that the borrower is actually using it for business purposes.

The usual contractual remedy would be to sue for the breach. The basic right to sue for the debt remains notwithstanding any other remedies that the lender might also enforce. However, there is an inherent problem with this remedy. Ordinarily you would expect the circumstances that lead to a borrower falling behind with mortgage repayments to relate to their financial position. A business failure or loss of employment, for example, might mean that there is simply not the money available to make the repayments. If this is the case, then suing the borrower for repayment of the debt is potentially unlikely to yield any financial compensation because the borrower does not have the money to start with. The lender may also, in this instance, be competing against other creditors who are also pursuing debts against the borrower.

The right to possession and sale

The most powerful remedy, then, against the borrower is the lender's right to possession of the property and, separately, the right of sale. These remedies flow from the fact that the property is used as security for the loan and the lender has rights that are equivalent to an estate in the land. The implications of these rights are in theory quite profound. In the famous case of *Four Maids v Dudley Marshall (Properties) Ltd* [1957] 2 WLR 931, Mr Justice Harman noted that *'the mortgagee may go into possession before the ink is dry on the mortgage'*. It would likely come as a shock to a house buyer to find that their lender has an immediate and automatic right to take possession of their property as soon as the mortgage is completed. The commercial reality is that a lender would have no intention of doing that because their only interest is in the loan and the interest payable on it. However, the right to possession remains an important and viable remedy that is generally only exercised as a last resort and in the vast majority of cases pursuant to a court order.

Where a lender applies to court for a possession order, the court may suspend or adjourn the proceedings if the borrower is able to demonstrate that they are likely to be able to repay the debt (or pay off arrears of instalments with a reasonable prospect that they will be able to continue to meet the repayments) within a reasonable period (the effect of s.36 Administration of Justice Act 1970). The courts have interpreted the reference to a 'reasonable period' quite broadly, even suggesting that what is reasonable is the remainder of the term. However, the borrower does need to be able to demonstrate a reasonable prospect of payment and if there are significant arrears and no apparent way to pay them off then the courts are likely to grant a possession order.

The subsequent right of sale is implied by statute. s.101 of the Law of Property Act 1925 gives lenders this right and implies it into mortgages that are made in the form of a deed (provided the deed does not expressly exclude it). In practice, this will cover the vast majority of mortgages as you will remember that to create a legal mortgage a deed has to be used.

The power of sale arises when the mortgage debt becomes due to be repaid. For this purpose the date that the debt becomes due is the legal date for redemption of the mortgage (which you will recall from earlier in the chapter is generally six months into the mortgage). Although we have said that the distinction between the legal and equitable rights to redeem have become blurred, it is common to see the legal date for redemption retained in mortgage deeds for this purpose. Once the date has passed, notwithstanding that equity will extend the rights of the borrower to repay, if there is default then the lender can pursue their power of sale.

The nature of the default that will lead to a lender exercising their power of sale is set out in s.103 of the Law of Property Act 1925. The lender has the right to sell the property as soon as the redemption date has passed *and* one of the following events has occurred:

1   the borrower has failed to repay the mortgage debt three months after the lender has formally demanded repayment; or
2   the borrower is at least two months in arrears with the interest payments; or
3   there has been a breach of some other provision in the mortgage deed.

The lender is under a duty to get the best price reasonably obtainable for the property and remember that they still also retain their other rights and remedies in respect of the property. If the value of the property has fallen since the mortgage was created so that the debt owed is greater than the value of the property (this is often referred to as negative equity), then the lender might exercise their right to sue for the remainder of the debt after the proceeds of sale have been applied.

Foreclosure and the appointment of a receiver

Foreclosure is a little used remedy that allows the lender to acquire the title to the property when the borrower defaults. Once title is transferred, the debt is extinguished and the lender loses the right to sue for any remaining sums due.

The appointment of a receiver might be made where the mortgaged property is commercial. The receiver receives rent or other profits from the property on behalf of the lender and uses these to pay off the debt that is due.

APPLICATION OF THE PROCEEDS OF SALE AND THE PRIORITIES OF MORTGAGES

Where a lender exercises their right to take possession and sell the property, the next consideration will be how the proceeds of sale will be applied. s.105 of the Law of Property Act 1925 sets out the order in which the proceeds of sale are paid and Figure 10.1 summarises this process.

The reference to 'priority' in relation to mortgages clearly relates to a situation where there is more than one mortgage in relation to the property and the order in which they will be

Figure 10.1 The application of the proceeds of sale following possession and sale of a property

paid. You would assume that the lenders would get paid based on the order in which the mortgages were created and this will often be the case, but only where following the creation of the mortgages they have been protected in the appropriate way. Regard must be had to how the mortgages, as interests in land, have been protected.

This is perhaps best explained by means of an example. We will start with the position relating to unregistered land. Imagine that an individual bought a house with an unregistered title in 1972 with the aid of a legal mortgage in favour of Lender A. Lender A protected their mortgage by taking possession of the title deeds, which they still hold. Subsequently, in order to finance some renovations to the property the borrower entered into a second legal mortgage in 1988 with Lender B. Lender B cannot take possession of the title deeds and so must protect this second mortgage by registration of a Land Charge (in this case it will be a Class C(i) Land Charge referred to as a 'puisne mortgage'). If, a year later, another third mortgage was created with Lender C but shortly afterwards the borrower defaulted and possession was taken and the property sold, then the order of payment would be Lender A, Lender B and then Lender C. If, however, Lender B had failed to protect their second mortgage by registration of a Land Charge then, assuming the facts were otherwise the same, following a sale Lender C's mortgage would take priority over Lender B's and Lender C would be paid first. This would be the case even if Lender C had failed to register a Land Charge and regardless of whether Lender C knew of Lender B's mortgage. This is the effect of s.97 of the Law of Property Act 1925, which essentially provides that the order of priority of mortgages depends on the order in which they were registered as Land Charges and not the order in which they were created.

In relation to registered land, the principles are exactly the same. The priority of mortgages will rank in relation to their registration as charges against the title and not in relation to the order that they are created. In the sample registers in Chapter 3 the dates in brackets indicate the dates on which the registrations were made. In that example, Weyford Building Society would be paid before Fast and Furious Building Society.

These rules highlight the importance of the adequate protection of mortgages as interests in land. Failure to protect a mortgage properly can result in a lender losing their priority and potentially large sums of money (not to mention the potential for negligence claims against their legal advisors).

MORTGAGES AS PART OF THE CONVEYANCING PROCESS

The detailed practice and procedures that must be followed when acting for buyers of a property with the aid of a mortgage, or indeed sellers who are redeeming their mortgage on a sale of their property, are outside the scope of this book. However, it is helpful to an understanding of the law relating to mortgages to appreciate a little of the process.

If you think back to the basic introduction to conveyancing process in Chapter 2 it should make sense that the interests of the lender largely mirror the interests of the borrower in terms of the checks that are undertaken prior to an exchange of contracts taking place and the eventual mortgage being completed. While the lender is not acquiring title to the property they are using the property as security for the loan that they are making and are acquiring a proprietary interest in the property. Therefore the seller's capacity to sell, any other rights or interests that might affect the property and any defects in the title are going to be as relevant to the lender as they are to the buyer/borrower. Ultimately, the lender will want to know that the borrower is going to acquire a good title to the property and that there is nothing that would affect the value of the property (and therefore the lender's security) or the ability to sell.

Solicitors acting for the buyer/borrower will, therefore, often also be instructed to act on the lender's behalf and this is generally allowed under the professional conduct rules that govern solicitors. Equally, solicitors acting on the sale of a property will generally be instructed by any existing lenders to use the proceeds of sale to redeem and discharge the existing mortgage on the property in order that the buyer can acquire title free from the legal charge.

Finally, solicitors acting for the buyers of property from a lender in possession will need to be aware of the lender's rights and remedies and ability to sell in order to ensure that their client acquires a good title. In that case the buyers' solicitors will need to check that the lender has a power of sale (remember that this is implied by s.101 of the Law of Property Act 1925 where the mortgage is made in the form of a deed), and that the power of sale has arisen. This last point takes us back to the legal date for redemption and the earlier comment that this date is still usually retained in mortgage deeds. The solicitor will check that the legal date for redemption has passed, meaning that the power of sale has arisen and their clients can acquire a good title from the lender.

SUMMARY

- Mortgages are proprietary rights in land, but come to an end when the borrower has complied with the terms of the mortgage.
- Mortgages are now protected by registration of a legal charge, created using the formalities of a deed.
- Borrowers are protected by the equitable right to redeem their mortgage against oppressive or unconscionable terms or undue influence.
- Lenders have a number of rights and remedies available to them in the event of borrower default, the most important being the right to possession and sale.

FURTHER READING

The Council of Mortgage Lenders Handbook: www.cml.org.uk/cml/handbook – sets out standard instructions for solicitors when acting for lenders in respect of a new mortgage and is a useful resource when considering mortgages as part of a conveyancing transaction.

Dixon, M., *Modern Land Law*, 9th edn (Routledge, 2014) – refer to this textbook for a more detailed review of the protection offered to borrowers and the rights afforded to lenders.

Greer, S., '*Horsham Properties Group Ltd v Clark*: possession – mortgagee's right or discretionary remedy?', *The Conveyancer and Property Lawyer* 2009, 6, 516–524 – a useful article that considers the rights of possession and the operation of s.36 of the Administration of Justice Act 1970 where the action is brought not by the original lender but by a third party purchaser.

The Law Society, Practice Notes on Mortgage Fraud: www.lawsociety.org.uk/advice/practice-notes/mortgage-fraud/#mf1_1 – this useful practice note sets out what mortgage fraud is and signs to look out for as well as suggesting steps that law firms can take to prevent this happening.

Richman, H. P., 'The Etridge Mortgage Cases: a review', *New Law Journal*, 151, 1541 – this article sets out a review of the judgments in Etridge and the guidelines given by the House of Lords in relation to undue influence.

Index